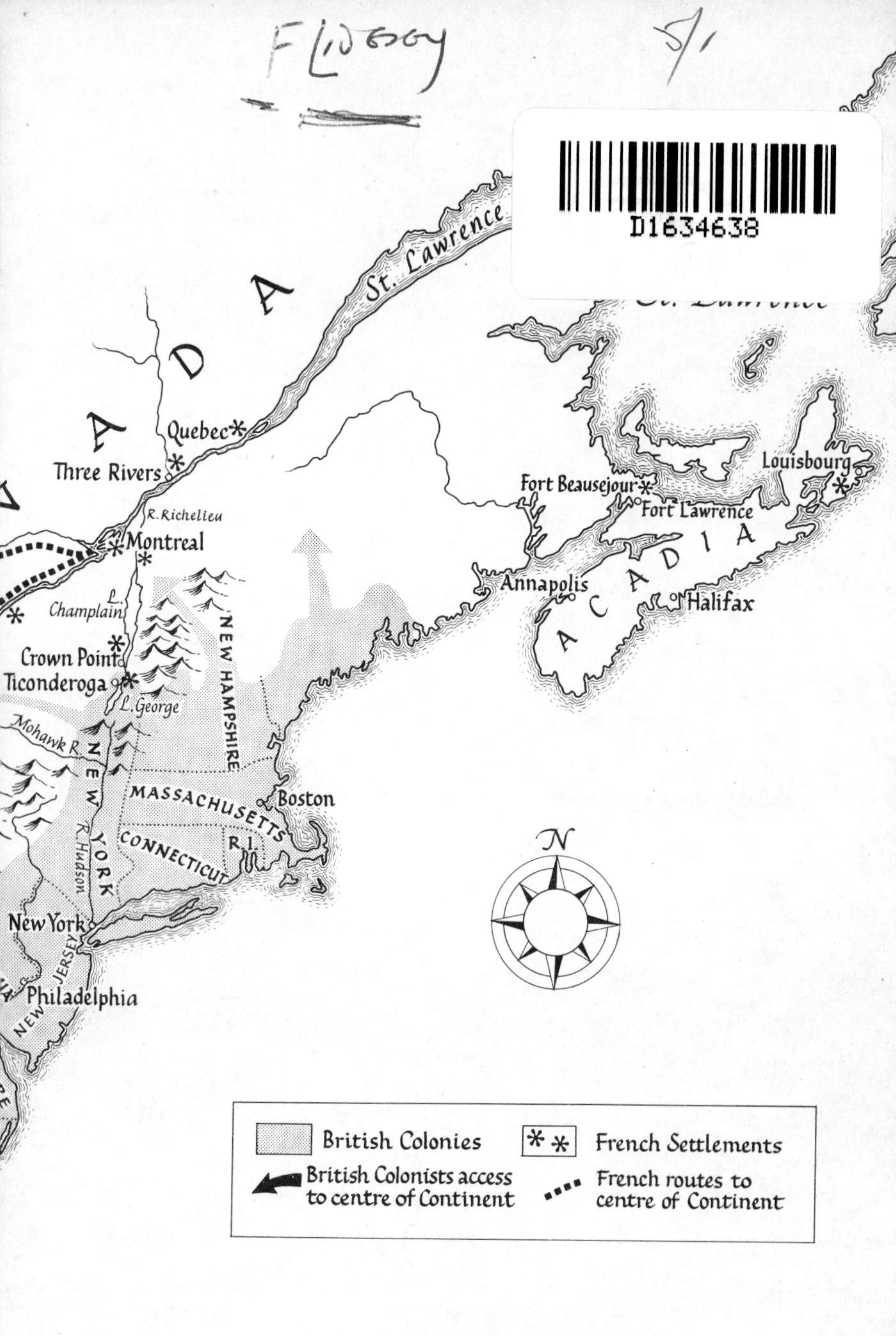
St. Lawrence
Quebec
Three Rivers
R. Richelieu
Montreal
L. Champlain
Crown Point
Ticonderoga
L. George
Mohawk R.
NEW HAMPSHIRE
NEW YORK
R. Hudson
MASSACHUSETTS
CONNECTICUT
R.I.
Boston
New York
NEW JERSEY
Philadelphia
Fort Beausejour
Fort Lawrence
Louisbourg
Annapolis
Halifax
ACADIA
N
British Colonies
French Settlements
British Colonists access to centre of Continent
French routes to centre of Continent
0 50 100 150 200 250
Miles
REGMARAD

THEN AND THERE SERIES
GENERAL EDITOR
MARJORIE REEVES, M.A. PH.D.

The Struggle for Canada

BARRY WILLIAMS

Illustrated from contemporary sources

LONGMANS

LONGMANS, GREEN AND CO LTD
48 Grosvenor Street, London W1
Associated companies, branches and representatives throughout the world

First Published 1967

TO ANN

ACKNOWLEDGEMENTS

The author wishes to thank the Librarian of Fort Ticonderoga Museum for her courtesy and help, and Mr. B. J. Clifton of the Rank Film Library for help in tracing the American sources of contemporary illustrations. The author would also like to acknowledge his debt to C. P. Stacey's *Quebec, 1759,* Macmillan of Toronto, 1959 and to E. P. Hamilton's *French and Indian Wars,* Doubleday, 1962.

For permission to reproduce illustrations the author and publisher are also grateful to the following: Fort Ticonderoga—pages 9, 24, 64, 72, 78 and 79; The Historical Society of Pennsylvania—page 28; Lord Egremont, Petworth House—page 103; The McCord Museum, McGill University—pages 56 and 99; The Marquis de Montcalm—page 49; National Film Board of Canada—pages 6, 14 and 17; National Life Insurance Company—page 30; National Maritime Museum, Greenwich—pages 89 and 100; National Portrait Gallery—pages 53 and 95; The New Brunswick Museum—page 70; The Public Archives of Canada—pages 50, 62 and 82; Radio Times Hulton Picture Library—page 42; Royal Canadian Air Force—page 93; The Royal Green Jackets—page 61; United States Information Service—page 4, and William L. Clements Library, Michigan University—page 33.

PRINTED IN GREAT BRITAIN BY
E. J. ARNOLD AND SON LIMITED
LEEDS

CONTENTS

TO THE READER

If you were asked to name the largest French-speaking city, Paris would be the obvious answer. But could you name the second largest? You will probably be very surprised to find that it isn't in France at all, but in Canada: it is Montreal, the huge city of over a million inhabitants on the St Lawrence River. Canada has 18,238,000 people, the majority of whom speak English. Today it is an independent member of the British Commonwealth of Nations. Most of its population live within a hundred miles of the boundary with the United States of America, so although Canada looks large on a map it is very thinly inhabited. These eighteen million people have made Canada an important country: it is the fourth trading nation in the world, with powerful industries and mining, and producing vast quantities of fish, furs, timber and wheat. The 1961 Census shows us that five and a half million, that is thirty-one per cent, of all these Canadians are descended from the original French settlers, and still live mainly in Quebec Province. French-Canadians are a powerful minority in Canada, and even today many of them are not happy living in a country dominated by people of English descent.

The story of this book tells how the French and the British fought a desperate struggle in the mid-eighteenth century for control of the main Canadian settlement area around the St Lawrence River and Great Lakes. Canada was not as prosperous then as it is today, but its French settlers were adventurous, and they looked like carving off a huge slice of North America for themselves. Unfortunately the British colonists wanted the same slice.

1 Washington at Great Meadows

Prelude to the duel for a continent

In 1750 the greater part of North America west of the Great Lakes and the Appalachian Mountains was uninhabited by white people. The St Lawrence River area had been occupied by the French and called New France; the eastern coast of America had been settled as separate colonies such as Virginia, Pennsylvania and Massachusetts mainly by English-speaking people. It was clear that soon both the French and the English would want to push further westwards and settle; they already knew something of this area because they were trading with the Indians who lived there.

In the spring of 1753 the French made a sudden move. The Marquis Duquesne (pronounced 'Dew-cane'), Governor of New France, ordered a thousand French soldiers from Montreal to the valley of the River Ohio. These men were to occupy the upper reaches of the river and build forts to make the region secure. By so doing, Duquesne argued, the Virginian and Pennsylvanian traders would find their route westwards cut, and the Indians of the valley would have to turn to the French only for their guns, knives, hatchets and clothing. A show of vigour and daring, the Governor felt, would bring the Indians on to the French side. It was a bold plan, and for a while it succeeded. But Duquesne's decision set going a train of events which was to change the entire history of North America.

The French expedition speedily crossed Lake Erie by canoe and landed at a point they called Presqu'île. Here they made a base, using its excellent harbour and completing a fort of chestnut logs—the first of a series of forts to be built, cutting deep into the Ohio country. From the coast a road was laid to

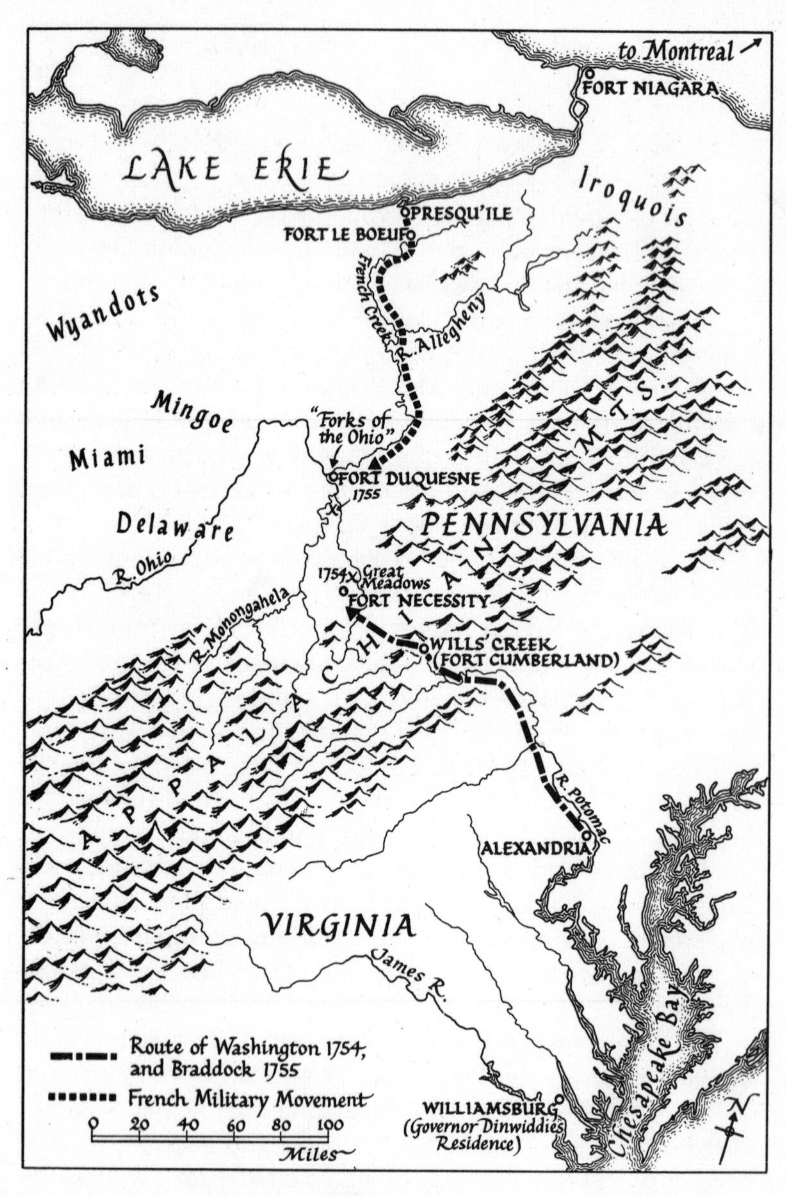

The contest for the Ohio Valley, 1754 and 1755

a small creek, inland, that gave an easy water route to the big Ohio river. At the head of the creek a second wooden fort, Le Bœuf, was begun. The Indians of the area behaved exactly as the Marquis Duquesne had forecast: impressed by the French move, some of the Miami tribes, for long close allies of the English, changed sides. But fever and scurvy hit the French, and they prepared to face the winter at Le Boeuf before making further headway.

Out of the forest, on 11 December 1753, a tall man on horseback appeared in front of the French fort. He had with him five white men and a few Indians. The journey had been a difficult one; they had travelled for six weeks through dense undergrowth and marsh, where heavy rain and snow had nearly destroyed the traders' trackways. The leader brought with him a letter from Governor Dinwiddie of Virginia:

> 'I express astonishment that Frenchmen should build forts on lands so *notoriously** known to be the property of the Crown of George II. It becomes my duty to require your peaceable departure.'

The letter also introduced its bearer as Major George Washington of the Virginian militia. This journey launched Washington at twenty-one years of age on the famous career that thirty-six years later made him the first President of the United States.

The French refused to move. Washington returned home to find that Dinwiddie did not intend to let matters rest; he had received clear instructions from the King in London: 'We do hereby strictly charge and command you to drive them off by force of arms.' This was easier said than done. Washington retraced his steps to the headwaters of the Ohio with only a small regiment of soldiers, and he was not happy about his chances. The Virginians in their local assembly had protested against the right of the British Crown to tax them to pay soldiers, and had only granted a very small sum for military

* Words printed in italics are explained in the glossary on page 108.

George Washington

purposes. So his force of three hundred was ill-equipped, ill-trained and difficult to discipline; it would stand little chance against an organised body of Frenchmen. But Washington's orders were definite: build a fort at the Forks of the Ohio. (The spot chosen is where the great industrial city of Pittsburgh now stands.) Forty men set about the work, but had hardly begun before a swarm of canoes came down the River Allegheny from Fort Le Bœuf. Five hundred French soldiers drove off the Virginians, and began to build their own fort. When finished, it was small but strong; they named it Fort Duquesne. This was the third French defensive point, and it was obvious to the English colonists that they were dealing with a powerful and determined enemy. A glance at the map will show you that the French had advanced a long way. They were now only sixty miles from the Wills Creek trading station, a vital one for the Virginians in their trading links with the Indians of the region. In an area as vast as North America such distances seemed comparatively tiny, so the Virginians felt the French were on their very doorstep.

Washington began immediate and serious preparations for another attack on the French. A road for cannon and transport wagons would have to be cut through forest and over mountain streams, and in April 1754 the work started. Only twenty miles were covered in the first two weeks. By the end of May Washington's men had reached a place called Great Meadows, which was on the west side of one of the main ridges of mountains. It was a level tract of grass and bushes with wooded hills around it. Here a halt was called, for news had come to Washington from some friendly Indians that a small advance party of less than fifty French was in the region. The Indians offered to lead Washington to surprise the French. The fight was short. De Jumonville, their leader, and nine other French were killed, and a score or so captured; only one man escaped.

What really happened, and who fired the first shot is hard to say. Washington kept a detailed journal in which he claimed that the French were hostile; the French say de Jumonville carried a flag of truce. An outcry of horror went up in France. Whatever really took place, this small, distant skirmish began an armed contest for supremacy in North America.

Washington paid dearly for his boldness. A thousand French, aided by Indians, left Fort Duquesne to take revenge. Expecting this, the Virginians worked hard to build a defensive stockade at Great Meadows. It was up in three days, and was aptly named Fort Necessity. When the French came a bitter struggle took place. It lasted nine hours. The last hours were fought in torrential rain, which became so heavy that it was impossible to fire a musket; bedraggled French and Virginians could do little but gaze at one another through a grey veil of mist and rain. A truce was arranged, but Washington decided to abandon his small fort, for he knew the odds were too great—he could not match the force of Duquesne's men.

The retreat from Great Meadows, back over the mountain road to Wills Creek, began. The date was 4 July, a day which Washington in another year was to help make famous, but at this time all he could think of was his hurt pride, and how by this defeat he had lost the confidence of the Indians in the area. This was important, for now Dinwiddie was forced to appeal to Britain for military help; when General Braddock and his regular soldiers arrived next year, they were to find that the Indians had already gone over to the French in the Ohio valley.

Before telling the story of the fate of General Braddock, we ought to pause and ask some questions. Why was this River Ohio worth fighting for? Who were these 'French' from Montreal? Were the Virginians fighting a lone battle? Who were the 'Redskins' the French were so anxious to get on their side? The next chapters will answer these questions for you.

The first trading post at Quebec, established in 1608

2 Problem: How do you fix a Frontier?

If you look up the word 'frontier' in the dictionary, you will probably find something like, 'a border between settled areas'. Before the white man came to America about 1500, the vast continent was the home of the American Indians, more popularly called Redskins. Their way of life was not 'settled' in the manner we understand the word; no exact borders existed between the tribes, although they did concentrate in certain areas. By 1700 French and British settlers also were well-established in the north-east part of the continent.

Colonists from Britain developed the coastal strip between the Appalachian Mountains and the Atlantic Ocean, and the colonies of Massachusetts, New York (taken from the Dutch), Pennsylvania, Maryland and Virginia were formed. Others could be added by going north-east or south, but at some point the climate became too cold or too hot for comfortable settlement. So, as the population of the British colonies grew (it was about one-and-a-quarter million in 1750), the obvious route of expansion was westwards. The best way was through a gap in the Appalachians which the Virginians used, and then down the River Ohio; this would take settlers a long way in the right direction.

The French had explored the St Lawrence River region. As long ago as 1608 an explorer named Champlain had built a trading post at the first good point up-river which ships could use as a harbour. The local Algonquin Indians had a word for this post, which means 'the closed-up place'. It is still known by this word today: Quebec. But, if you were an explorer, you would not be satisfied until you went further up the river—just to see, as it were, what lay beyond the next bend. If you look at the cover map, you will see three ways of getting from Quebec to the heart of North America and the great Mississippi River. First, there is an easy but long route: Quebec—Ottowa River—Lake Superior—Upper Mississippi. Secondly, you could use the Great Lakes and cut across from the southern tip of Lake Michigan to the Mississippi. Thirdly, the shortest route and the one the French wanted to use, was to go up the St Lawrence, across the lakes Ontario and Erie, and join the headwaters of the River Ohio, which flows into the Mississippi in the centre of the continent.

Can you see the trouble which would result? Both British and French expansion westwards would lead to a clash in the region of the upper Ohio.

Perhaps you can see a second important point. What have all these routes in common? The answer is 'water'. The choice of travel by land or water in those early days in North America was really no choice at all. Think of carrying all your equipment—blankets, axes, food, guns—for hundreds of miles over land with no tracks and much mountain and forest! A pack-horse might solve your equipment problem, but the bare mountains and forest leaves would give a poor diet for the animal, so forage would be yet another item on your list. Instead you would use the great waterways of the continent.

By 1750 two main types of boat had been developed. There was the birch-bark canoe, the gift of the Indian to the white man. It was extremely light, had a shallow draught, and could easily be repaired if damaged; it could take about 500 lb of goods. For the bigger tasks a bateau was used. None has survived from those days, but we have a record of several bateaux being used on the Mohawk River in 1750: they were 25 feet long, 3 feet 3 inches wide and 2 feet deep; each could carry a score of soldiers and their 1500 lb provisions for about thirty days. They were not difficult to build, and six men in a hurry could make one in a couple of days.

Over the years certain places became well used as portage points for carrying these boats from one river or lake to another. Some you could guess at by looking at a map—Niagara Falls, between the lakes Ontario and Erie, was one. Then there was the 'Great Carrying Place', linking the River Hudson with the lakes George and Champlain. These two lakes are in an enormous trench through the Appalachians; it is four hundred miles long, and nowhere rises to more than a hundred feet above sea level. A route such as this would be valuable to trader and soldier alike, for it took a fortnight only to move along it. At the northern end stood the French town

Bateaux at a portage point

of Montreal; at the southern end, New York, the British colonists' town. As our story develops we shall see that control of this passageway became vital to both sides.

This chapter started by using the word 'frontier'. To make a settled and peaceful border, both sides must agree on where it is to run. But ask yourself this question: what standard or test should be taken if there is a dispute? To whom in America did this inbetween-world of mountain ranges, forests and swift-flowing rivers belong? The French could stake a claim by right of discovery and occupation. But, even in 1750, the whole population of New France numbered only 55,000. The British colonists were rapidly growing in numbers, and were afraid of being hemmed in by a vast arc of French forts, which might stretch from Quebec to New Orleans, at the mouth of the Mississippi.

The British colonists feared the French, but they feared each other also. Each colony jealously guarded its own rights. The governor of Virginia, Robert Dinwiddie, wrote a letter to the British government in London in October, 1752: 'Till the line is run between the two provinces, I cannot appoint magistrates to keep the traders in good order.' The 'two provinces' were Virginia and Pennsylvania. Uncertain ownership was the great evil that bred suspicion and open war. And although the main British colonies saw that they must get possession of the Ohio if they wanted to expand westwards, they hesitated to join together against the French. Dinwiddie, in 1754, made an urgent appeal to the colonies to meet at Albany, in New York, 'in order to defeat the designs and intrigues of the French'. Few turned up.

As we have seen, such hesitation was fatal. The incident at Great Meadows proved that the French were already one step ahead of the British. They had struck hard and effectively at the Ohio Valley. If the conference table could not bring an agreed frontier, then force would have to be used.

3 New France: its Rulers and People

New France, or Canada, was a French colony with small settlements along the banks of the St Lawrence River. Life there was closely controlled by the powerful King of France; he could not, of course, directly rule a country three thousand miles away from his court near Paris, so he personally appointed his own officials. However, instead of one chief official there were two, and they often quarrelled violently. First, there was the Governor, whose real power, in spite of his title, was over the army and the Indians; the second man, the Intendant, had the usual powers you expect of a governor—such as keeping law and order, making quick decisions, and administering the taxes and expenses of the country. In fact these men were only servants, whose main duty was to put into practice orders received from France; but you can imagine that as the Intendant controlled the money of the colony, and made decisions on the regulation of inns, the sale of alcohol, the value of coins, etc., there was plenty of opportunity for fraud. If the Intendant was a rogue, the lesser officials of New France became more like a gang of thieves. Bigot, the Intendant during the 1750s, was such a man.

New France was a feudal colony. This meant that the king leased out land there to *seigneurs*, who in turn leased some of it out to tenants. Some of these seigneurs formed a sort of upper class, the 'noblesse' (this does not mean nobility—the nearest English word would be 'gentry'); but others of them were very poor and of humble origin. The Canadian tenant called himself a *habitant*, and was certainly much better off than he would have been living in France itself. He was not a peasant in the European sense, because his life was fairly free; many of the harsh laws of the Old World hardly existed in Canada.

C. W. Jefferys drawing from the Imperial Oil collection

Habitants paying their yearly dues in money and goods to the seigneur

Frontier life needed muscle, not manners, and the habitant's standard of living depended very much on the amount of hard work he was prepared to do. Ambitious men had everything in their favour, and they became the backbone of the colony. A typical land-grant looked like a ribbon, a few hundred yards wide and one-and-a-half miles deep, with one end on the river and the other on the uplands behind, so that a tenant might have some good meadow and some forest for timber. The French Canadian community was a very close one, and original grants were side by side, each with its own river frontage. However, as generation succeeded generation, land was often subdivided, and with it the river frontage. There were some peculiar results, and one story tells of a certain point on the St Lawrence where one enormous elm tree used to shade the frontages of three farms!

Generally, rural life was fairly satisfactory. There was plenty of fuel—a great attraction for people coming from France where it was limited. There was also much to eat: bread and pork in plenty, and at least two menus became so traditional that today they could be called national dishes: pea soup, and pork-and-beans. But remember, the population was small; if it was increased very quickly, food would have to be shipped from France because the area of farming land was only small.

Life in the few towns was also pleasant enough in the early eighteenth century. Quebec was a gay little capital with a population of about 4,500. Montreal was a smaller community of the frontier. One governor of New France recorded that on a visit he saw two hundred known thieves in the many gambling and drinking houses. But this was about 1700; by mid-century it had grown larger and prosperous on the fur fair profits.

In both towns there was plenty to show the power and importance of the Catholic Church in people's lives: besides churches there were convents, monasteries and schools run by the clergy. But there were no printing presses and few books.

The wealth of New France came from the fur trade, and we shall see later that this was a severe handicap when it came to expanding the numbers of the colony. There were few industries—a little iron was smelted at Three Rivers for utensils and stoves—and, although government officials talked of developing products like hemp and pitch they never came to anything. What about the famous Canadian timber? Some small efforts had been made to encourage the timber trade for shipbuilding; as far back as 1669 we have a record of 'three new ships made of local timber' which were anchored off Quebec. But the French government and merchants of the early eighteenth century simply failed to understand the enormous possibilities that Canadian timber had. They preferred to make the quick profits to be had from, say, the West Indian sugar trade. Also, as one governor was heard to say, 'The small number of inhabitants causes every enterprise to fail.' There were many reasons for the smallness of the population. Seventeen years of bitter warfare with the Iroquois Indians had cost New France the lives of many men; disease, like the smallpox epidemic of 1703 in which 2,000 died, was another. So Canada was really a forest with a narrow edge for its 18,000 people in 1700; even by 1750 this number had only risen to a mere 55,000.

A roadway was opened in 1734 to link Quebec and Montreal, but travel down-river was still mostly by water. In 1749 a Swedish explorer named Peter Kalm took this journey, and has left us an interesting account of what he saw and heard. A habitant's farmhouse was made of stone and clay walls, two feet thick and well whitewashed. 'Near each farm', says Kalm, 'there is a kitchen garden in which onions are most

A pioneer farm in New France

abundant. The common people in Canada may be smelled when one passes by them on account of their frequent use of onions.' The house was really only one room, with an iron stove and a floor of clay or wood; what furniture there was, was made up of table and chairs, although Kalm noticed that in some poorer houses wooden boxes were the only things to sit on, and windows were covered with paper. Children slept in the attic, which was reached by climbing up a ladder and through a hole in the ceiling.

The people of New France faced long winters cut off from the outside world. The regular arrival of ships from Europe ceased when the winter cold froze the St Lawrence; this ice would not break until perhaps April of the following spring. The evenings of these long winters were taken up by a round of visits, for the inhabitants lived close together; there was plenty of opportunity to meet socially for dancing, folk-singing and story-telling based on old colonial legends. Pipe-smoking was also common, for Kalm tells us that, 'It is likewise very necessary that one should plant tobacco, because it is so universally smoked by the common people. Boys of ten or twelve year old run about with pipes in their mouths, as well as old people.'

On special days in the year the habitant and seigneur might meet: on 11 November (St Martin's Day) the seigneur sits at a long table to receive his tenants' land rents, usually in the form of small amounts of cash, wheat bags and live chickens. Then on 1 May a big festivity is held at the *seigniory*. At daybreak the 'Mai' or maypole is made by chopping down and stripping the branches from a spruce tree; then, at a small ceremony, the habitants drink the health of their landlord, and for the next half an hour muskets are fired at the 'Mai'—by tradition the blacker it is made the more honour that is paid to the seigneur. Feasting and festivities continue until noon in three rooms set aside for eating: one for the seigneur and his family and the oldest habitants, a middle room where all the food (meats, vast tarts, maple sugar cakes, wine and brandy) is piled high on a table, and a third room where the young people of the area eat, sing and shout.

Kalm said some interesting things, not all of them complimentary, about the women and girls of Canada. They worked hard in the fields, but 'they seem rather remiss in regard to the cleaning of utensils and apartments, for sometimes the floors, both in town and country, were hardly cleaned once in six months'. In Montreal,

> 'the women are handsome here; they are well bred and virtuous with an innocent and becoming freedom. Their hair is always curled, powdered and ornamented with glittering bodkins and *aigrettes*. Every day but Sunday they wear a little, neat jacket and a short petticoat [skirt], which hardly reaches half way down the leg, and in this particular they seem to imitate the Indian women. The heels of their shoes are high and very narrow.'

On the question of marriage the position at Montreal was much worse than at Quebec. Kalm tells us why.

> 'The girls at Montreal are very much displeased that those at Quebec get husbands sooner than they. Many young gentlemen who come over from France with the ships are captivated by the ladies of Quebec and marry them.'

Peter Kalm did not think these Quebec girls deserved this advantage. They were lazy, and although they seemed to do some needlework, they

> 'place themselves near a window that opens into a street, and turn their eyes into the street most of the time. When a young fellow comes in, whether they are acquainted with him or not, they immediately lay aside their work and chat, laugh and joke.'

Earlier in the century there was a great shortage of women. Louis XIV had seen to it that a regular shipment of men had added to New France's population; but the new settlers wanted wives, so some nuns from French convents began organising expeditions which took girls also out to the colony. Some people at the time made spiteful gossip out of this, and one evil-minded Frenchman named La Houtan told of halls in Quebec packed full of girls, where

> 'the bridegrooms chose their brides as a butcher chooses his sheep, for here were to be seen the tall and the short, the blonde and the brown, the plump and the lean.'

Some recent writers have found such stories were very exaggerated. A 'matrimonial market' certainly existed, but girls were allowed to reject any suitor who displeased them.

The King's Girls: French-Canadians choosing their wives from girls newly arrived from France

For some men the opportunities to get on were not enough in the small towns and immediate countryside. So another group grew up, apart from the seigneurs and the habitants. The French called men in this third class *coureurs de bois*; they were fur traders, adventurers and explorers. The King of

France and his officials in Canada bitterly disliked these men, for they refused to fit into the orderly life of the colony. Young men, the most active and vigorous in the community, took to the woods in great numbers. Around 1700 one of the French governors wrote: 'It deprives the country of its effective men; it makes them *indocile*, *debauched* and incapable of discipline.' He goes on to describe how, on return from the forest areas, the coureurs de bois 'swagger like lords, spend their gains in dress and drunken revelry, and despise the peasants'. This, of course, was only one point of view. If asked, these men would have given a much more favourable view: they saw themselves as 'bushrangers' with a daredevil courage and reckless gaiety, and it was a cruel king who tried to stop their natural movement to the woods. But try he did. A law was passed saying: 'Any person going to the woods without a licence should be whipped and branded for the first offence, and sent to the *galleys* for the second'.

You may wonder what made the forest so attractive. It was the little beaver. European fashion had made the beaver-fur hat very popular with the well-to-do classes—in fact it became a sort of badge of social status. The skin itself was not used, but the 'beaver wool', a fine, short under-fur, was taken off the skin and felted into a hat. The demand was for large and expensive-looking hats, and somehow it had to be met. In the early days, the Indians with their long cloaks of beaver were an obvious source. As the demand grew, the Indians would be persuaded to come to the French settlements with skins by promises of great feasting and drinking; big annual fairs like the one at Montreal became established. Then French traders found the English were trying to cut off their source by going into the forest themselves; so the French did the same. They became great experts in the beaver trade, and in the early eighteenth century New France exported about 150,000 skins a year, as against the English colonies' meagre 8,000. The

French built forts as they moved deeper in to the forest, and slowly a chain of these extended up into the Great Lakes region.

Not that the French always made the profit they expected; it could be three years between the time a trapper decided to go into the forest and the time he saw the money for his work. And complete reliance on the beaver had a serious disadvantage. Convinced of the enormous wealth to be gained, so many trappers produced so much fur that the market became flooded: the price of hats went down, and so did the profits. Once, the hat fashion in Europe changed and a smaller hat was favoured; you can imagine the unemployment and misery this caused in a New France virtually dependant on the profits of the fur trade.

Also, the British were not to be put off for ever, and in the first half of the eighteenth century many traders from Albany, in New York colony, began pushing into the Ohio valley area, and furs that normally had gone to Montreal and Quebec went to the ports of New York and Boston. The following table will show you how successfully the British had been undercutting the French in a price war for the Indians' beaver.

The Indians must give	*In Boston*	*In Montreal*
for 8 lb musket powder	1 beaver	4 beavers
,, 1 rifle	2 ,,	5 ,,
,, 1 red cloth blanket	1 ,,	2 ,,
,, 4 shirts	1 ,,	2 ,,
,, 10 pairs stockings	1 ,,	2 ,,

By 1750 the French Governor, the Marquis Duquesne, began to take stern measures to safeguard his people, and a contest between the British and French began in earnest. Perhaps you can see now why those thousand French soldiers were sent from Montreal to take control of the Ohio River.

4 The British Colonists: their Hopes and Fears

Although in the end the struggle for Canada was decided by two professional armies trained in European warfare and supported by large fleets, in the beginning the conflict was between two very different sorts of colonist. We have seen what life was like in New France; a brief glance at the thirteen British colonies will show some important differences. The enormous one of population has already been mentioned: the British had a twenty-to-one advantage. But the French had a single government, with one master, the king, while the colonies had thirteen separate governments called assemblies. These assemblies had no ties with each other except a common allegiance or bond to the British Crown. There was no such person as a patriotic American colonist: the country of the Virginian was Virginia, the Pennsylvanian, Pennsylvania, and so on.

Most of the people living in these colonies had British ancestors—English, Scots, Welsh or Irish—but there were many others with a different background. The Negro slaves made up twenty per cent of the population, and there were also Germans, Dutch, Swedes and Jews who had come to form this gigantic 'melting-pot' of immigrants from the Old World of Europe. Their way of life, however, was clearly British and their language mainly English.

Around 1750 these colonies could be divided into four groups, and between each group many important differences existed, pointing contrasts with themselves and with the French. The southern colonies included Georgia, the Carolinas, Virginia and Maryland. Nearly half the Virginian population was Negro, and these slaves were used on the big tobacco plantations. Although the tobacco crop was the most famous one in the south, it was far from being the only one: rice and *indigo* in South Carolina and iron-mining in Maryland were very important. The big plantation owners lived comfortably in large and elegant mansions. You might say they were just like the English aristocracy—but there was one important difference. Their position depended on riches in land and slaves, not on being born with a title and a high position in society.

A talented Virginian named William Byrd II kept a diary which we still have; in it he showed himself to be a typical example of the cultured, powerful southern 'aristocracy'. He kept in close touch with the mother country, England, where his father had sent him to be educated. By sheer hard work he turned his plantation into a prosperous business, and founded what the English would have called a '*baronial seat*' on the James River. Byrd was very cultured: he had a library of 3,600 books, liked to think of himself as something of a doctor and a scientist, and his diary records that he got up many times at 3 a.m. to read Hebrew, Greek or Latin until breakfast. Over the years he prospected for coal, iron and copper on his land, built a large and profitable sawmill, and became a tobacco merchant. He certainly worked hard, but he also drank heavily, and gambled away the evenings at dice and cards. He was one of the many rich colonials who *speculated* in land, and saw the vast possibilities of the 'west' as an area to develop both for trade and settlement, for, as a young man, he had become rich by trading pots and pans, guns and rum with the Indians of the Appalachian Mountains.

George Washington's family also saw that a man could gain wealth and keep an upper-class position in society by developing new lands. So you can see one more vital difference between the Virginian and the Canadian: Byrd, Washington and others were not so hampered by government restrictions as the

French were. There were few towns in the south, but Charleston, a small one of about 10,000 people, had a public library, bookshops, a newspaper, milliners who kept up with the European fashion, social clubs and even a race course.

Go north to Philadelphia, and you would find yourself in the second city of the whole British Empire; for here was a place more prosperous than even New York or Boston. It was the home of merchants, shipmasters, shopkeepers and craftsmen, who together formed a wealthy and powerful middle class. It was here that the famous Benjamin Franklin made his reputation as publisher of the 'Pennsylvanian Gazette'. In these 'middle' colonies some great centres of learning—schools, academies and universities—were built. The Academy opened its doors in 1751, and offered an excellent education to the sons of prosperous families; five years earlier, one of today's famous American Universities, Princeton, had its first college built in New Jersey colony.

Cross the River Hudson, and you will be in the New England colonies, which formed a third distinct group. Here the people were almost entirely descended from Englishmen, and in some cases from the original Pilgrim Fathers. Known as 'Yankees' by the other colonists, this was a remarkably successful group of people. As traders, on land and sea, they had a reputation for working hard, looking after their money shrewdly and resisting outsiders who tried to interfere with them; Massachusetts, for example, was practically an independent country.

Inland from the coast and the towns of all these colonies was an area that became known to Americans as the 'Frontier'. Here was a small farming community, which made up the fourth region, and its men and women were jealous and watchful of the wealthier coastal merchants and planters. They were men of great energy and adventure, and were the nearest equivalent to the *coureurs de bois* or trappers of New France.

Several of them became important colonial citizens, after founding their fortunes on trade in furs or with the Indians.

These thirteen colonies were under the control of the Crown and Parliament in London—in theory. But in practice only a few of them had much to do with the king's government. The

C. W. Jefferys drawing from the Imperial Oil collection

An eighteenth-century print showing Indians trading furs at a store

Penn family, for instance, ruled Pennsylvania like a piece of personal property until the American Revolution. Also, the English government's aim of reducing the number of colonies (to make the administration cheaper and defence against the French and Indians easier) came to nothing. The mother country controlled trade and relations with foreign countries, but in matters of taxes, laws, voting and local government positions, the colonies were in full control.

A French Canadian might envy the British colonists for their individual freedom, their larger colonial population and greater wealth. But could these thirteen colonies agree on a common plan of campaign against the French? We have seen in Chapter 1 how soon Dinwiddie had trouble with the Virginian assembly. The French had a more efficient leadership in the early years of the struggle. A central authority, better relations with the Indian, even better trained and regular soldiers were other French advantages.

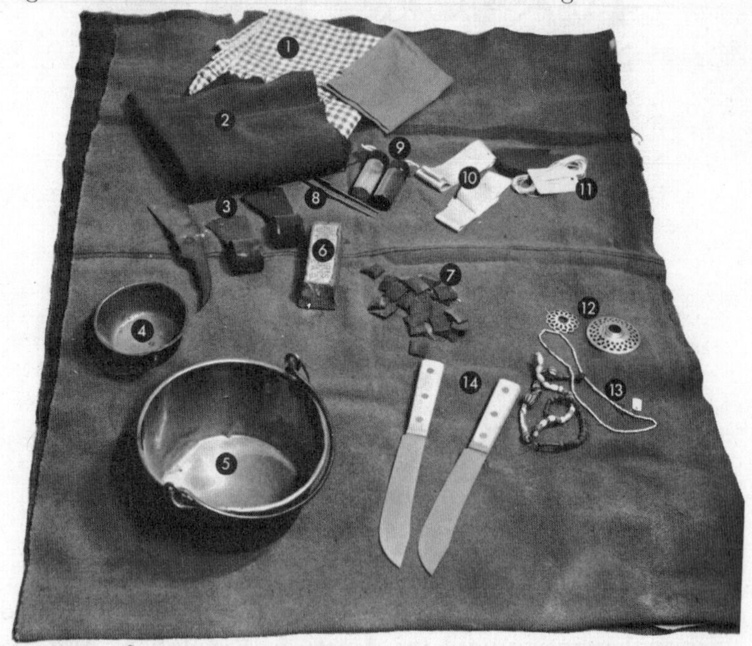

A collection of original goods traded with the Indians, now displayed at Fort Ticonderoga Museum

Key

1. Checked shirting. 2. Wool shroud. 3. Axes and tomahawks. 4. Small brass kettle. 5. Larger brass kettle. 6. Bar lead. 7. Gun flints. 8. Awls. 9. Vermilion containers. 10. Bright ribbon. 11. Needles and fish line. 12. Silver ornaments. 13. Wampum beads. 14. knives.

5 The American Indian in the Struggle

Imagine a man of the Stone Age suddenly being given a chance to use firearms: this is what happened to the American Indian. By European standards you might think he was primitive and savage. Nevertheless, he had a civilisation of his own, and because this Indian played a part in the struggle for Canada between France and Britain, it is worth while taking a look at his way of life. In appearance all American Indians look similar: straight black hair, copper-coloured skin (hence 'Red' Indian), a prominent jaw and a hooked nose, rather like an eagle. Yet there were many different groups, divided from one another by spoken language and types of government. In the north-east of America, around the Great Lakes and Appalachian Mountains, there were two main groups: the widely-spread Algonquins and, like an island in their midst, the powerful, more advanced and warlike Iroquois.

The white man had many things these Indians wanted—all the varied products of an industrial Europe, like woven cloth (gaudy, scarlet stuff was in great demand), knives, guns and kettles. The Indian had some things the European wanted—furs and deerskins. An immediate trade sprang up. The Iroquois developed a profitable business acting as 'middlemen': they were the go-between in the task of getting furs from the Indian tribes further west, and bringing them to the English traders at Albany.

The Indian received two other things from the white man that destroyed his way of life for ever: they were liquor and disease. The traders soon found the Indian had a craving for strong alcoholic drinks like French brandy and English rum, and would do anything to get them. There were no half measures in the Indian's drinking, and when drunk he was quite uncontrollable. A missionary in the 1750s wrote:

> 'Any time in the night if we awoke we were obliged to hear the songs of drunken Indians. A barbarous, doleful noise you know it is. We saw Indian women and children skulking in the adjacent bushes, for fear of the intoxicated men.'

Disease had devastating effects on tribal numbers. The American Indian had never come into contact with some of the germs brought by Europeans, and he had no bodily resistance to them. In an epidemic like smallpox thousands would die, and tuberculosis produced havoc in some tribes.

The Indians did not form a united opposition to the menace of the white man's advance westwards. Tribal rivalry was very common, and the warlike nature of some groups of tribes like the Iroquois caused much bitterness. About 1650 the Iroquois, driven on by greed and desire for conquest, began a savage war with the surrounding Algonquin tribes. In forty years of bloodthirsty conflict the Iroquois reduced the once formidable Hurons to a mere hundred or so fugitives.

Let us take a look at the social life of the American Indian. The Iroquois, for example, were nearing the end of the fishing and hunting stage of primitive development, and many of the tribes were no longer nomadic. Sometimes called the Five Nations, the map on page 2 will show you roughly where the main group of Iroquois were concentrated. Where they settled they built fortified villages about five acres in size. A dry, three-foot ditch was dug around the village, and a vast timber defensive line made; on top of the fence of stakes heavy bark sheets were laid for the defenders to stand on. Inside this defence the huts were scattered all over the place.

If you have in mind a picture of the wigwam, with its conical framework of poles, as the only Indian home, then you may be interested to know that the Iroquois used to live in large huts. They were about thirty feet in length, breadth and height; many were very much longer—240 feet in some villages. The frame was of tall and strong saplings, planted in a double row to form the two sides of the house, bent till they met, and lashed together at the top. To these, other poles were set and bound crosswise; the whole thing was covered with large sheets of bark—elm, oak or spruce—which overlapped like roof slates. At the crown of the arch and along the entire length of the house, an opening a foot wide was left to let in light and allow the smoke to escape. At each end of the house a small room was added to keep stores. Inside, long planks, about four foot up from the earth, were covered with skins and used as beds. There were several fires burning, for the hut would house more than one family. Clothing, weapons etc. were hung from poles suspended from the roof.

There was not much privacy for the Indian, and we have many records, left by white visitors, which tell of the appalling smoke and fleas. The smoke especially was bad, because it pricked the eyes and produced inflammation; many Indians were partially or totally blind as a result. Cooking, eating and gambling occupied most of the long winter nights, with each hut a noisy collection of old and young men, shrivelled squaws and highly decorated young women, many children and dogs. By 1750, things were changing: separate log cabins were slowly replacing these long-houses, but some remained, holding as many as twenty families each.

Land was not usually owned separately by each family, but an area of land could be kept for a family's own use for a year or so, on condition that they cleared it. This clearing was a long process—you can imagine the task of cutting down a tree with only Stone Age tools. The way it was done was to hack off branches, pile them at the foot of the tree and then set fire to them; the charred stumps and earth were later hoed with bone and wooden tools, before sowing corn, beans, tobacco, sunflowers and hemp (a plant like a mulberry). The main food would be Indian corn; as it was cooked without salt, we would find it rather tasteless. Meat was eaten, and dog-flesh and venison were thought to be great luxuries. The squaws worked hard to feed their large families, and the Iroquois women were more advanced than some of their neighbours: earthen pots were made, before trading brought them French copper pots; also they knew how to get oil from fish.

Dress varied considerably. In summer, men of some tribes were naked except for moccasin shoes, but on ceremonial occasions they covered themselves from head to foot in valuable otter or beaver furs. The normal dress for women was much more modest: skins and wampum in abundance.

A fine example of Indian wampum

Wampum was the American Indian name for perforated beads which were made from the inner parts of some shells. They were strung in a variety of forms—belts to honour treaties, or more usually for personal decoration like necklaces. There was also a great deal of variation in the hair style. Some had it closely matted on one side of the head and loose on the other; others had the famous shaven head with a hair-ridge running across the crown. Tattooing was a common and painful process; when the whole body was covered, many Indians died. The body-painting was done with the juice of berries, or soot and white clay.

You may wonder how so-called savages could live together in their close-knit communities with reasonable harmony; white men have described them as vain, boastful and showing a ruthless cruelty to an enemy; they could not be relied upon, and were often greedy and thievish. But within their tribal organisations they had a strong code of honour and a hospitality to friends that amazed white men. Law as we know it did not exist; there was a kind of common law, based on various customs, but there was no jury or court to see that it was kept. Murder and witchcraft were regarded as the worst offences, yet even these were really matters for the family to settle. If an Iroquois was killed, then his family received gifts from the murderer's family, with a very formal ceremony.

The Iroquois had a government which could never be described as primitive. The most important chiefs were called *sachems*, and there were fifty of them who ruled the Iroquois Confederacy, or group of tribes. They gathered together at a central point in the Confederacy (on a modern map of New York State, you will find it marked as Syracuse), and discussed their problems in a very orderly fashion: no speaker was ever interrupted by another, and no decision was ever rushed into. A French Jesuit priest named Lafitau, who knew the Iroquois well, wrote a description of one of the meetings:

> 'It is a greasy assemblage, sitting on their backsides, crouched like apes, their knees as high as their ears, or lying, some on their bellies, some on their backs, each with a pipe in his mouth, discussing affairs of state with much coolness and gravity.'

The life of women and girls was a curious mixture of freedom and drudgery. In some tribes, women could own property, and the Iroquois had women's councils that sent opinions to the Grand Council of Sachems. Marriage, at least as the European knew it, did not exist; yet a form of family life was set up by a man and woman making an agreement, and sealing it with a gift of wampum. An Indian girl could change her husband at any time—and frequently did, before she settled down with a permanent partner! Then life became very dull and monotonous: sowing, tilling, harvesting, and preparation of food. When an Indian tribe moved to a new area, 'their

'The American Indian had an evil reputation for cruelty'

women', said the French explorer, Champlain, 'were their mules'. Is it any wonder that the old squaws looked like shrivelled hags?

The American Indian on the warpath was an alarming sight. White men have left us accounts which vividly describe why. Father Roubaud, a French missionary, wrote:

> 'Imagine a great congregation of savages, decorated with all their ornaments, most capable to the European eye, of disfiguring one's appearance: vermilion, white, green, yellow, black, made with the scrapings of soot from the cooking pots—the face of a single Indian unites all these colours.'

Colonel Bougainville, of the French army, told his brother:

'Indians, naked, black, red, howling, bellowing, dancing, singing the war song, getting drunk, yelling for 'broth'—that is to say blood—drawn from five hundred leagues away by the smell of fresh human blood, and the chance to teach their young men how to carve up a human being destined for the pot. I shiver at the frightful spectacle which they are preparing for us.'

Before we accept completely such a description as this, we must remember that, as the Indians left no written records, our view relies on the opinions of white men, many of whom were totally hostile to their way of life. Yet it is still true that the reputation of the Indian in war was hideous. By the 1750s, the evil side of many an Indian had been made worse by the liquor trade. Iroquois cruelty was proverbial: settlers and soldiers told hundreds of stories of the most appalling ferocity. Dr Caleb Rhea, a British army surgeon, described it in his diary:

'I can't but take notice of the cruel nature of our Indians. When they took a prisoner their custom was to confine him, and making a ring around him, scourge him with whips or prick with sharp pointed sticks, tearing his nails out by the roots, scalping alive. They would shout and yell like so many fiends.'

Such was the ally of both Frenchman and Briton. Certainly the Indians could not be depended upon. As the struggle for Canada developed, they became less important. In the next chapter, you will see them play a vital part in the story, but by the end of the book, when the fighting between the British and the French reaches a climax, Indians are hardly mentioned. General Wolfe at Quebec refused to employ them, calling them 'a dastardly set of bloody rascals'.

6 Braddock 'gainst All Disaster

During the evening before he left London for America, Edward Braddock, newly promoted to Major General, said to Anne Bellamy, 'I am going with a handful of men to conquer whole nations.' Miss Bellamy was a childhood friend, and perhaps Braddock thought such a brave remark suited the occasion. But the next months were to prove just how unsuited Braddock himself was for the task before him. Horace Walpole, a gossip writer of the day, said of Braddock: 'He was brutal in his behaviour, obstinate in his sentiments.' We shall see that his one virtue, courage, was to be of little use to him.

On 14 April 1755, in a tent at the Alexandria military camp on the River Potomac in Virginia, Braddock read out to an assembled council of colonial governors the instructions he had received from the British government. Dinwiddie's appeal for help had been answered, for the French were to be attacked at several points. Braddock himself, aided by Washington, was to take two British regiments and some colonials to seize Fort Duquesne; Crown Point, vital to the control of the Hudson Valley, was to be captured by Colonel William Johnson, the energetic Indian Superintendent from New York colony; and in Acadia Colonel Monckton, a quiet but efficient regular officer, was to seek out the French in their stronghold at Fort Beauséjour, which controlled the narrow neck of land at the head of the Bay of Fundy.

On paper this was a worthy scheme. If you are wondering how the British in London could justify such warlike blows in peacetime, you must remember the frontier difficulties, and the failure of Washington's three journeys into the Ohio River region. By now questions of right and wrong had been lost amidst a mass of claims and counter claims. The British government simply insisted that the forts to be taken were actually on soil belonging to the British Crown—the French were merely trespassers. You must decide for yourselves whether the British had right on their side, or whether their argument was only a useful piece of moral humbug—that is, a cover to hide their real designs against the old enemy, France.

General Edward Braddock

Braddock faced difficulties at once. Dinwiddie was eager, but feared that, as in the previous year, his assembly would not be willing to provide the money to keep the campaign going. His worst fears were soon realised: supplies of horses, wagons, forage and food were scarce locally, and no one seemed keen to provide them. Braddock became furious with impatience. At the last minute about two hundred wagons arrived, sent urgently from Pennsylvania by Benjamin Franklin. With these the expedition was able to set out for Fort Duquesne. (Look back to Chapter 1 for a map.)

Early in May 1755, then, Braddock gathered his force at Wills Creek. The old Indian trading station, which Washington had previously used as a base, was now fortified with log ramparts and ten small cannons, and had been renamed Fort Cumberland. The lessons of the previous year's failure had been learned: Braddock was not going to venture into so-called enemy-held territory, and be caught without an established supply line. But he was very worried about the quality of his troops; some he could depend on, but also included in the 2,200-strong force were 500 Virginian recruits, whom he called 'slothful and unfit for military service'.

The expedition started on 10 June. Eight days later, it had advanced only thirty miles. This was not because the leaders were too cautious, but because they found the country appallingly difficult to cross—it was a waste of lonely forest and mountain. Three hundred men had to axe their way forward, whilst the wagon-train lurched behind along a road less than twelve feet wide, over stumps, roots and stones. The line of march sometimes extended back for four miles. One American writer has given a vivid description of it as

> 'a thin, long *party-coloured* snake, red, blue and brown, trailing slowly through the depth of leaves, creeping round inaccessible heights, crawling over ridges, moving always in dampness and shadow, by rivulets and waterfalls, crags and chasms, gorges and shaggy steeps. In glimpses only, through jagged boughs and flickering leaves, did this wild, *primæval* world reveal itself, with its dark, green mountains flecked with morning mist and its distant summits pencilled in dreamy blue.'

Later there were other reasons for Braddock's slow progress. Fever broke out amongst the men, and they had to be left at the several supply dumps; the horses became very weak on their diet, which was mainly of leaves. Then, as the attackers neared the fort, Washington complained to Braddock about the care taken in 'levelling every molehill, and erecting bridges over every brook', instead of boldly pressing on. So it was 8 July before a main force of about 1,200 men came within reach of its target.

Fort Duquesne, commanding the route westwards down the River Ohio, was a small but solidly built square construction. It had water close to two sides and prepared ditches on the other two; also it had ramparts of logs some twelve feet high, with earth fillings ten feet thick. An enemy would find it hard to capture. Yet, with Indian scouts providing detailed information to the fort's commander, the French were determined to ambush the British before they could even mount an attack.

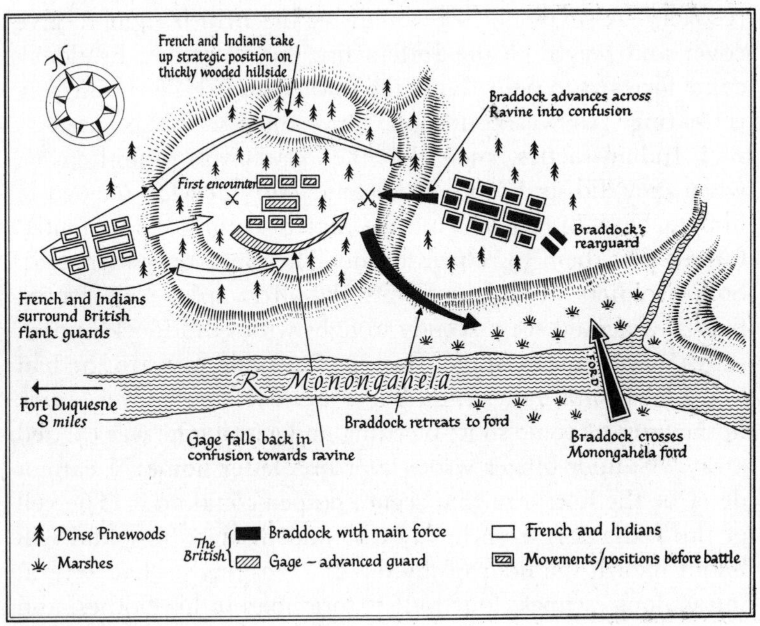

Braddock's defeat 1755

About six hundred Indians and three hundred French were ordered along a track leading to the River Monongahela, where the British were crossing.

But the plan of ambush did not work out, and there was no surprise when, on 9 July, Braddock's advanced guard under Colonel Thomas Gage met the French and Indians in heavily wooded country about eight miles from the fort. Gage had the better of the struggle in the opening minutes. His men quickly moved into battle formation and opened fire: although little damage was done, the noise in the enclosed forest was deafening, and some of the Canadian militia turned and fled. The Indians, however, vanished behind the thick cover. Then, while the British stayed on the open track firing volley after volley into the forest blackness, the remaining French officers rallied the Indians, and ably led them into a dramatic recovery. A small hill was found on the British right to give cover and height to the Indian fire, so that when Braddock came forward to help Gage, the soldiers in front were already retreating. All was confusion. Only the Virginians, used to such Indian tactics, knew that the answer was to find cover; when they did so, Braddock became angry at what seemed to him to be a breach of courage and discipline, and shouted furiously at them to return to line. The panic only increased. Some soldiers complained bitterly afterwards: 'We would fight if we could see anybody to fight with.' Braddock himself showed immense courage. Dashing back and forward, he had four horses shot under him. On a fifth occasion he was struck in the lung by some shot; bleeding and gasping he was carried away. A junior officer wrote later in a letter home: 'I cannot describe the horror of that scene; no pen could do it. The yell of the Indians is fresh in my ear, and the terrific sound will haunt me till the hour of my death.' Washington had several miraculous escapes: four bullets tore holes in his clothes, and he lost two horses. He made efforts to rally his troops, but

Courtesy of Chicago Historical Society

The dying Braddock retreating from the battlefield

'with as much success as if we had attempted to stop the wild bears of the mountains', he said afterwards.

The battlefield was abandoned three hours later to the noise and plunder of the Indians. Over sixty officers and 700 men of the original 1,200 were killed or badly wounded. The French lost only ten men; the Indians, the real victors, scarcely a hundred. The appalling story of rout and ruin was brought back by the British survivors to Fort Cumberland, sixty miles distant. Braddock died on the way—at 8 p.m. on Sunday, 13 July. Before dying, he murmured, 'We shall better know how to deal with them another time.' He was buried immediately, and the wagons ordered to roll over his grave to remove all traces, for fear the Indians should find and mutilate his body.

Was Braddock to blame for the disaster? His name and reputation were viciously attacked by many people in England, when the news arrived. Perhaps they were looking for a *scapegoat.* But some eyewitness accounts give a more favourable picture. Washington disliked Braddock as a man, but was very impressed by the handling and organisation of the force. Charges that Braddock walked blindly into an ambush seem to have no foundation, as he made careful preparations to prevent surprise. Gage, perhaps, should have seen how important that small hill was, and seized it himself. Braddock had plenty of courage, but obviously he was the wrong man for the job: trained to fight in Europe, he had no answer to the Indian methods of fighting.

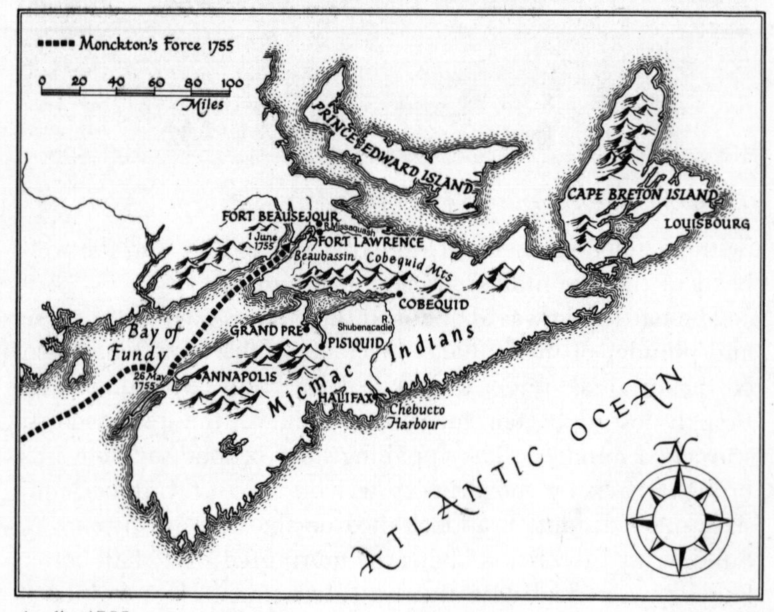

Acadia 1755

7 Acadia: a Hollow Victory for Britain

If you look at a map of Canada today, you will see the province of Nova Scotia on the extreme eastern tip of the country. This used to be the French settlement of Acadia. It became British territory in 1713 by the Treaty of Utrecht. This treaty had one very special sentence in it: the French of Acadia were 'to enjoy the free exercise of their religion according to the usage of the Church of Rome'. This meant that, although they were to be ruled by a Protestant king, they could go on worshipping freely as Roman Catholics.

The British thought they were being generous, but peace and order never came to Acadia. Three things prevented the French Acadians and their new British rulers from getting on with one another.

First, the Catholic priests, who were controlled by their bishop in Quebec, were an energetic group of men, and they saw to it that their parishioners still thought of the King of France as their true master. The British obviously disliked this.

Secondly, the British decided that their tiny garrison should be strengthened. A new settlement was to be built, to offset the importance of Louisbourg, the powerful French port and fortress a mere fifty miles off the north Acadian coast. For the new settlement a good harbour was found on the Atlantic coast, and in 1749 what is today the great city of Halifax was established. In three years its population was 4,000. The French in Canada and in France were alarmed, and they began using a local Catholic missionary to stir up the Micmac Indian tribes against the British. The missionary was Joseph le Loutre, a vain and violent man with an intense hatred for the new rulers of Acadia; the British put £100 on the head of this 'good-for-nothing scoundrel'. It was to le Loutre that the Marquis Duquesne wrote in October 1754: 'I invite you to devise a *plausible pretext* for attacking the English vigorously.'

Thirdly, the old frontier question was never settled. By the Treaty of Utrecht Acadia was British. But what was Acadia? The British said it was the peninsula and all the land to the north as far as the banks of the St Lawrence. The French said Acadia was really only a narrow belt along the Atlantic coast of the peninsula. Between these two extremes was a neck of land called Beaubassin, at the head of the Bay of Fundy. Both sides decided to seize control of this neck of land. In 1750 Major Lawrence took over the Beaubassin region, and built a fort there, which he named after himself. But he had only a few troops, and was unable to prevent the French from establishing themselves in another fort at Beauséjour: it was only three miles from Lawrence's small defensive point. The English and French faced each other with mounting hostility.

If you remember, the plan which Braddock brought from London said a second objective was to capture Fort Beauséjour. The fort's commander was named Duchambon de Vergor—a rather stupid man, 'of no education, of stuttering speech and unpleasing countenance', said a man who knew him. With Vergor was le Loutre. These two men were certainly not the finest choices to defend the honour of France against attack.

On 1 June 1755 a small fleet and 2,000 volunteers from Massachusetts, commanded by Colonel Monckton, arrived in front of Beauséjour. Monckton was a cautious man, and he decided to take a few days getting his camp ready and bringing up his artillery in preparation for a long siege. While this was going on, some skirmishing took place with the French. Suddenly, before Monckton had even put his heavy cannon properly in place, a stray English shell hit the fort, and fell through a roof on to some French officers, who were having their breakfast. The shell exploded, killing six. Both Vergor and le Loutre were in another room a few yards away; they were terrified and immediately ordered the white flag of surrender to be raised on the ramparts. Some of the regular officers present protested violently at Vergor's easy capitulation, but in vain. Beauséjour surrendered. Meanwhile, le Loutre quietly slipped away before the English entered the fort, and made his way to Quebec. He was well aware of the price the English had put on his head!

But Monckton's victory had a hollow ring about it, and the sequel was tragic. The English were still suspicious of the Acadians: did they really keep a personal loyalty to the French King Louis XV? The Acadians were asked to take an oath of loyalty (or 'allegiance' as it is called) to the King of England; yet only a few families turned up for the ceremony. The English feared a rebellion, and were exasperated at the lack of cooperation they were getting from the Acadians. Finally, the English governor announced that:

> 'Your lands and houses and cattle and livestock of all kinds are forfeited to the Crown with all your other effects, except money and household goods, and that you yourselves are to be removed from this province.'

In the next six months, 6,000 men, women and children were put on transport ships, and sent to different parts of North America, as widely separated as Massachusetts and Georgia. Others, after incredible hardships, reached the French settlement at New Orleans in Louisiana. Not all Acadians left quietly: some escaped to Canada or lurked in the dense Acadian woods, waging guerrilla warfare against the English.

8 The Battle of Lake George

In Chapter 2 you read how important was the 400-mile long trench between Montreal and the town of New York. Both the English government and the colonial leaders saw the danger of the two watery routes of attack, Lakes Champlain and George, pointing like a rapier at the British settlements. The French already had an advanced post at Crown Point on Lake Champlain; the New Yorkers felt much the same way about this post as the Virginians did about Fort Duquesne. So the capture of Crown Point became a key aim of the 1755 campaign, and the third big objective in the plan which Braddock brought with him.

The commander of this expedition was to be William

Sir William Johnson

Johnson. He was, in some ways, an odd choice, having never been in an army and knowing nothing about warfare. But he had one vital qualification: he understood Indians and, unlike many traders, treated them with justice and honesty. He was a tall, rough-looking man, ambitious and energetic. When he was planning the expedition he appealed for help from the neighbouring Indians of his home in the Mohawk River valley. Eleven hundred turned up, feasted and talked and drank the health of the King of England. But despite Johnson's influence, they seemed less willing to fight; only 300 Indians joined Johnson's force as it gathered in the Hudson Valley. Nor were the other men regular soldiers—they were farmers mostly, who had volunteered for the summer campaign. But there were plenty of them: 4,500 in fact. Their appearance was most unsoldierlike, but at least they had guns, and in place of bayonets they carried hatchets in their belts.

News of Braddock's defeat came just before they started out; and some Indian scouts brought rumours of 8,000 Frenchmen moving to reinforce Crown Point. Neither piece of information damped their spirits, as Johnson's men marched north to do battle. They followed the River Hudson to the 'Great Carrying Place'; here some men began to build a small supply base. The others pressed on, along an old Indian trail to Lake George, thought by many people to be the most beautiful lake in America. Even Johnson's force was very impressed, and everything had an air of leisure about it. Here is an extract from a diary kept by one of the officers:

> 'We stopped about noon and dined with General Johnson by a small brook under a tree; ate a good dinner of cold, boiled and roast venison, drank fresh lemon punch and wine.'

Johnson decided to camp at the southern end of the lake and wait.

Meanwhile, the French force prepared to surprise Johnson.

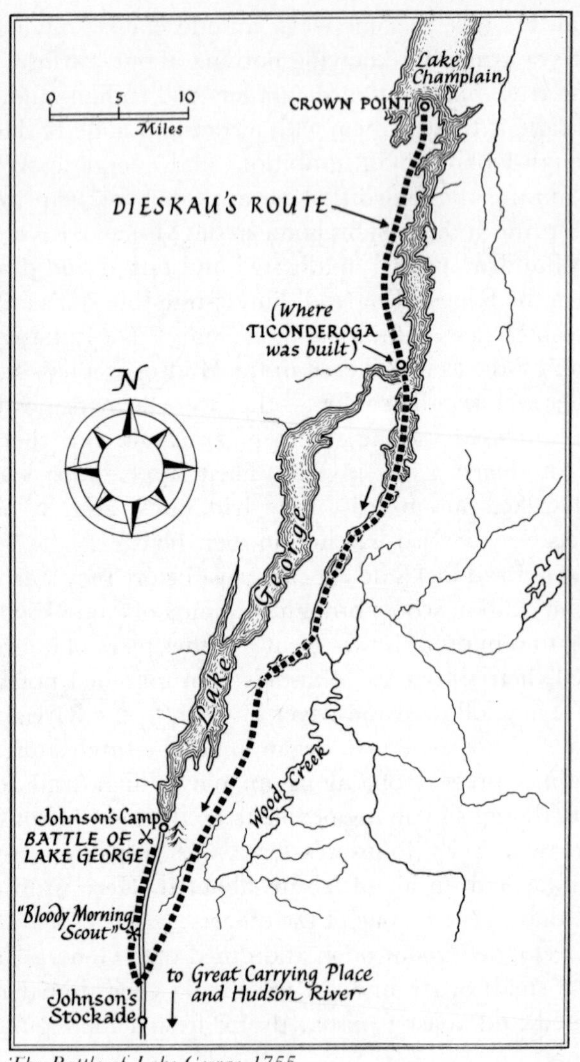

The Battle of Lake George 1755

It was led by a German soldier-adventurer, Baron Dieskau; he had 3,500 men, including Indians, a much smaller force than the rumours had said. As Dieskau moved south from

Crown Point, he had trouble with his Indians. He wrote in a report:

> 'They drive us crazy from morning to night. There is no end to their demands. They have already eaten five oxen, as many hogs, without counting the kegs of brandy they have drunk! In short, one needs the patience of an angel to get on with these devils.'

Early on 4 September, an English prisoner was brought in by a French scouting party. Threatened with Indian torture, he invented a story: Johnson, he said, had withdrawn, leaving only a few hundred men at his camp. Dieskau moved at once; by midday his force was already in canoes rowing down towards the colonials' camp. He landed on the east shore, and struck through the dense forest. Within three days he had a striking force of 1,500 near the enemy, but he had lost his chance of surprise.

Johnson's Indians gave him good warning, so he decided to send out a small detachment to meet Dieskau. It was a foolish thing to do, and showed how inexperienced Johnson was; the Indian chief told him, 'There are too few', and offered to let 200 of his greased, painted and befeathered warriors join the detachment. But the affair was badly bungled at the start: no advance guards were sent forward, and Dieskau had plenty of time to lay an ambush. It seemed as if Johnson's men were going to suffer the same fate as Braddock's. Dieskau sprang his trap, and in his words, 'the enemy was doubled up like a pack of cards'. There was blind panic for a few moments; but then the New Englanders took to the trees, and showed what Braddock's men should have done: in a contest with Indians, fight like Indians. Realising they were out-numbered, an orderly and beautifully handled retreat took place, and so ended the 'bloody morning scout'.

It was Dieskau's turn to behave foolishly. He came on, although his Indians became sullen and unmanageable at the thought of more fighting against their own kind. Johnson, by this time, had organised a good defence with rows of logs, and the struggle which followed—the Battle of Lake George—became a famous victory. A man who was there described the opening:

> 'The French Canadians and Indians, helter-skelter, the woods full of them, came running with undaunted courage right down the hill upon us, expecting to make us flee. Our chief officers threatened instant death to any of us who should stir from his post. Hailstones from heaven were never much thicker than their bullets came; but blessed be God! that did not in the least daunt or disturb us.'

The outcome became a matter of firepower—who could fire hardest and longest. For four hours both sides blazed away. Dieskau led three big assaults against Johnson's men, all in vain. Another was being prepared, but it was too late. The

Courtesy: Glens Falls Insurance Company, Glens Falls, New York

The men from Massachusetts at the Battle of Lake George

New Englanders crossed their rows of logs, and fell on the French with hatchets and the butts of their guns. The final rout was taking place. The French fled in disorder back to their canoes.

However, Johnson did not follow up his success. His men dispersed to their villages and farms, and Crown Point remained untaken. But the fame of William Johnson spread: Parliament in London gave him £5,000, and King George II made him a baronet. For where the experienced Braddock had failed, this raw young man had succeeded: the French had been halted on the field of battle.

During the battle Dieskau had been wounded and captured. This meant that the French regular troops in America were without a leader. To take over command, there came from France a man who was to become one of the most famous in Canadian history. His name: the Marquis de Montcalm.

Tait McKenzie's splendid statue of Wolfe

9 1756: New Plans and New Men Appear

Although you have been reading about a great deal of fighting, Britain and France were not yet at war officially. Perhaps if I say they pretended to be at peace, you will understand better. So far the most energetic men in fighting the French had been the colonials, like Dinwiddie and Washington and Johnson. These were men who served the colonies well in the early days of peril. However, you must remember that the French were showing themselves to be far more active: at Duquesne they commanded the water route of the Ohio; they were strengthening their hold on the Lake Champlain area; and Louisbourg, the guardian fortress at the entrance to the St Lawrence, was still firmly French.

Opinions were now changing—new men were entering the struggle, and the governments at home in London and Paris were beginning to take the situation more seriously. 1756 was a key year in the contest:

- — in that year, war was officially declared between Britain and France;
- — in that year, the brave and efficient Marquis de Montcalm came to Canada;
- — in that year, a great man, William Pitt (later Earl of Chatham) rose in power in the English government;
- — in that year, trained, professional British soldiers and sailors began the long job (which took 4 years) of making Britain the superior military power in North America.

Let us look, for a moment, at these new men—the commanders and rank-and-file on both sides—who were to give the struggle its epic quality.

Marquis de Montcalm

The French

On the French side three leaders stand out. First, the Marquis de Montcalm, who was appointed to command the French regular soldiers in New France in January 1756. He was forty-four years old, and was to prove himself the finest leader of men New France ever had. He was a small man, with a nervous temperament—this made him get angry very quickly. But he was completely honest, something unusual in those days. To his junior officers and men he must have been a very pleasant man to work with, for apart from the occasional angry outburst, he was generally cheerful, affectionate and civilised. He will always be remembered as a gallant figure in Canadian history. In our story we shall see him make many mistakes, and he was not a military genius; but his two famous images (in his shirtsleeves, urging his men on to the French victory at Fort Ticonderoga in 1758, and a sad, doomed figure on the great black horse re-entering Quebec in 1759) show why his legend is still a very powerful one. The last letter he wrote home to his wife is also famous and adds to his popular appeal:

> 'I think I should have given up all the honours to be back with you, but the King must be obeyed; the moment when I shall see you again will be the finest of my life. Goodbye, my heart, I believe I love you more than ever.'

Montcalm refused to suffer fools gladly: he did not have much time for weakness and incompetence, especially in his superiors.

Chief among these, and our second important leader, was the Marquis de Vaudreuil (pronounced 'Voe-dray'), who replaced Duquesne as Governor in 1755. If you met him, you would think he was a pleasant and rather mild person, but you would soon find out that he was not a man to have as an enemy.

Marquis de Vaudreuil

Ambition and jealousy were two features of his personality which made good relations with Montcalm impossible. Vaudreuil was a French-Canadian by birth; he had been born in Quebec in 1698, and his father had been a governor of New France earlier in the century. His experience of soldiering was very small, and he had never actually led a large body of men into action. Yet this was the man to whom King Louis XV gave supreme authority in Canada. He was not an evil man, although many writers in the past have seen him as the 'villain of the piece', because he turned a blind eye to the dishonesty and fraud of the Intendant and other government officials. Montcalm resented being placed under such a vain and pompous man. What Montcalm thought of Vaudreuil can best be seen by reading Montcalm's diary; during the struggle for Quebec in 1759, it said in one place:

> 'M. le Marquis de Vaudreuil, Governor-General, and in this capacity General of the Army, made his first tour of Quebec's new defences; after all, youth must be instructed. [Vaudreuil was 60!] As he had never seen either a camp or a work of defence, everything seemed to him as new. It was like a man born blind who had been given his sight.'

A bitter hatred developed between these two men which was not going to help the French win the war.

The third leader was Colonel Louis Antoine de Bougainville, only twenty-nine years old, but an interesting figure. He was despised by Vaudreuil, who called him a 'creature of Montcalm's'. If you saw him, you probably would not be impressed: he was short and rather fat. But he had a brilliant mind: he had already written a book on integral calculus, a very difficult kind of mathematics. In America he was to prove himself an able commander of soldiers. After the war, he became a famous explorer: on his travels in the Pacific Ocean, he brought back to Europe the 'bougainvillea', an exotic, tropical flower, and also gave his name to one of the

Solomon Islands, not far from Australia.

The troops these men commanded were of three sorts: the regular, professional soldiers from France, the Canadian colonial army and the militia—the ordinary citizens of New France who could be called on to fight. The first were the best. There were 3,500 of them, and they were under Montcalm's personal control. The other two came under Vaudreuil, but they were not anything like as highly drilled and disciplined as the regulars. Montcalm and Vaudreuil quarrelled because the command was split, and also because they disagreed on how best to use the men. Montcalm was a cautious soldier, who realised that the British had vastly superior numbers at their disposal; so he wanted to fight a defensive war. But Vaudreuil demanded a bold, attacking policy; so he sent Bougainville to France to ask for more troops. He returned with a mere three hundred. The French government kept its 100,000-strong army in Europe for the struggle that was going on at the same time with Frederick the Great of Prussia.

The British

The government in London had a very different view of the war. William Pitt controlled the overall direction of the war (or 'Grand Strategy' as it is called). He saw America as the key to success. Britain's ally, Prussia, was to keep up the offensive against the French in Europe with the aid of British money, whilst the major British effort took place against Canada.

Late in 1756 Pitt forced his way into power: for years he had accused King George II's government of failing in its duty. The King disliked him, but Pitt was not to be stopped; the English people were very dispirited, because their armies and navy had suffered many defeats in North America, India, Europe and on the high seas. Pitt told a friend: 'I am sure that I can save this country, and that nobody else can.' So, on 29 June

William Pitt, Earl of Chatham

1757, one of the most successful governments in British history was formed; in it Pitt had sole direction of the war. With enormous personal energy he shook the British people into action, and within a few months the *morale* of the whole nation changed. Huge sums of money were browbeaten from parliament, and Britain's naval and military power was reorganised to crush the French. Frederick the Great made this comment: 'England has long been in labour, and at last she has brought forth a man.'

Briefly, Pitt's plan was to use the navy and army as a single weapon: a sword, with the army as the blade and the navy as the hilt. England's naval power would be used, first to blockade the French ports, and stop supplies from crossing the Atlantic; and secondly to help the army in coastal operations. This may not seem very stirring or dramatic work, but you must not think that the only task of a navy is to win battles at sea. If it could cut off New France from the mother country, then, Pitt argued, the struggle was half won—remember that New France was small, and its prosperity and strength depended on keeping close ties with France.

To carry out Pitt's plan, there were many first-class naval officers: Admiral Hawke kept a long watch on the French ports; Admiral Boscawen took a huge fleet and a vast army to America; Admiral Saunders faced the difficult problem of getting a big naval force up the St Lawrence River. At the Admiralty was Lord Anson who overhauled the navy, planned new ships and, for once, saw that seamen's wages were paid on time. In 1747 Anson wrote his book, *Additional Fighting Instructions*. In it he showed his dislike of the customary methods of fighting at sea, in which a battle was fought by a massed attack; this seemed to Anson to be too much like safety-first. So he now encouraged bold and daring ideas by single ships. The new spirit in the navy is well shown by a story about Admiral Boscawen: once, in the middle of the night, he was woken by an officer, who said, 'Sir, there are two large ships which look like Frenchmen bearing down upon us. What shall we do?' Boscawen clambered up on deck in his nightshirt, and cried, 'Do, damn 'em, fight 'em!'.

The following diagrammatic map will show you a simple form of the plan which Pitt worked out for the army. Only the initial letters of the main places are given, so you must check them against the big map on the endpaper.

In theory, the plan was to work this way:

To be seized in 1758:

Ticonderoga (T) which blocked route to Montreal (M)

Louisbourg (L) on British right flank, and controlled

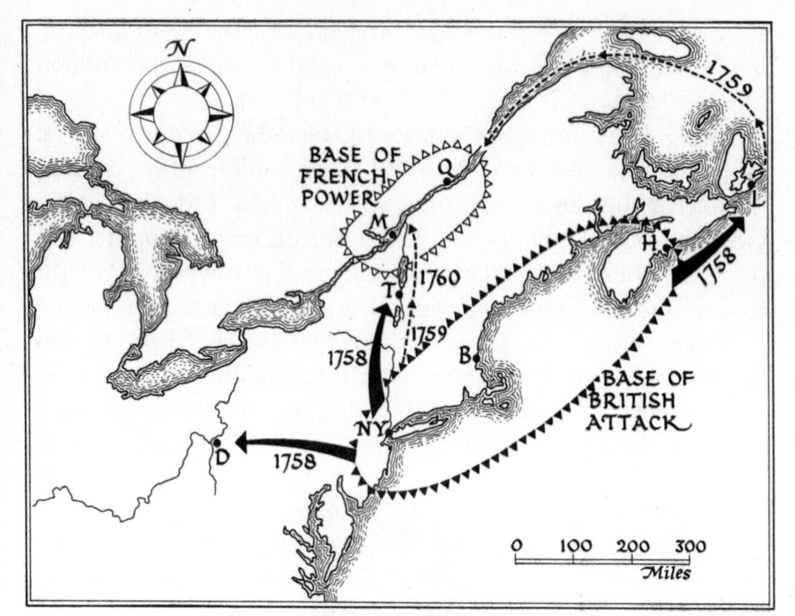

Pitt's plan for the defeat of the French

entrance to St Lawrence River
Duquesne (D) on British left flank

To be seized in 1759:

Montreal (M) } the base of French power. If they fell
Quebec (Q) } New France would no longer exist.

In practice, the plan did not quite work out: Ticonderoga only fell in 1759, and Montreal was not captured until 1760.

To put his plan into operation, Pitt's aim was overwhelming superiority in numbers and good leadership. 20,000 British regular soldiers were sent to aid the 22,000 colonial volunteers being assembled in the colonies in North America. To lead these men, Pitt had many able commanders. Take the brilliant Howe family, for instance; three brothers served the British flag with great distinction in the American struggle. The eldest, Lord George Howe, we shall meet at Ticonderoga;

Richard Howe was at sea, and later became the great admiral of Nelson's time; and the youngest brother was with Wolfe at Quebec.

Two names, however, stand out. General Jeffrey Amherst was a curious mixture of personal energy and military caution in face of the enemy. Perhaps this was why Pitt chose him. Give the man a good army and powerful naval support, Pitt thought, then Amherst's iron will and perseverance might steamroller the French into submission. Pitt was not far wrong.

James Wolfe was a more interesting figure. How do you think Wolfe measures against your ideal soldier? First, look at the portrait below. You would be disappointed in his physical appearance, which was far from impressive. Although over six

Brigadier Townshend's pencil drawing of Wolfe

feet tall, he was thin and lanky, with narrow sloping shoulders. His face would probably catch your eye: from the front it was thin, with high cheek bones, and he had a firm-set mouth and blue eyes; from the side, however, the appearance was unusual—a sloping forehead, a long nose and a double chin. His hair was red and usually covered with a wig. Wolfe was often ill, and it is thought that he suffered from tuberculosis: his brother had already died of it, and his many letters home to his mother complain about the effects of the severe climate on his health. Why then did Wolfe have such a hold over his men? He was still only thirty-two years old, and very much the idol of his soldiers. Two qualities made up for any drawbacks in personal appearance: they were the determination to succeed, which made him an inspiring leader, and his courtesy and charm in the company of others. Look particularly at Tait Mackenzie's sculpture on page 47, which many people think gives the best likeness to Wolfe. You will see all the peculiarities, but the details can be forgotten under that great impression of dignity, thoughtfulness and resolute determination.

These were the leaders; what about the junior officers? A modern army historian has said that at Quebec Wolfe was supported by 'probably the finest body of English officers, which has ever taken the field of battle'. In the struggle for Canada, this was a fact of supreme importance, and some credit for it must go to the British royal house—to George I, to George II and to the Duke of Cumberland. Over many years, these men had insisted that, instead of the usual practice of buying a senior rank, a man had to show he was trained for the position as well; they saw that proper discipline was enforced, and that promotion was given to young officers who showed keenness.

10 And what about the Common Soldier?

There was little that was romantic and glorious about a soldier's life in the eighteenth century. The British *regulars* were often from the very poor or even the criminal classes. Officers would sometimes visit gaols to offer freedom to prisoners in exchange for service in the army. The fact that these men became good fighters was largely due to their officers; it was an enormous advantage to have trained, professional men, who took a pride in their job, to command them.

The colonial soldier was looked down on by the 'regular'. British colonial units were made up of farm labourers, fishermen and the out-of-work, and they had no proper training. Their leaders were not much better, because to get a senior officer ranking you had to know someone in the colonial government. Some of the officers were squires, innkeepers and merchants, who were given commissioned rank (that is, made an officer) virtually overnight. We have seen that Braddock thought of these men as 'unfit for military service'. Nevertheless, there were some very good colonials who used a great deal of commonsense in dealing with a crisis. A third kind of military grouping was the colonial rank-and-file commanded by professional British officers. A famous one, the Royal American Regiment (which is still in the British army as the King's Royal Rifle Corps) proved that colonial troops could become excellent soldiers when given proper training and discipline.

Perhaps the greatest problem facing the officers was not commanding their men in battle, but keeping them occupied during the long months between battles. Training, road building and fort construction proved the best idea, but many of the rank-and-file still became lazy and dirty. An officer's notes on one British fort in July 1756 read:

> 'Men extremely indolent and dirty. Fort stinks enough to cause an infection. They bury five to eight daily from disease. Their necessary houses [lavatories], kitchens, graves, places for slaughtering cattle—all mixed through encampment; a great waste of provisions.'

In the diary of a chaplain at the same fort, we find: 'I pity our sick in their tents; on the ground with but one blanket. They are dying every day.'

This reference to disease may make you wonder what army medical care was like a century before Florence Nightingale. It was not good. A regiment of 600 men could count itself lucky if it had two doctors; attempts were made to provide hospital treatment, even when the troops were out in the forest areas. The army was not, of course, all male. A number of women went with an army—wives, launderesses, a few nurses. But there was a dark side to this picture: many soldiers, wounded in battle, were left to recover on their own, and 'bleeding', a favourite remedy in those days, could make matters worse. Medical treatment without proper anaesthetics and antiseptics meant that operations could be very dangerous, and often fatal. 'The bloody flux' (a form of dysentry which caused serious diarrhoea) was by far the most common disease, and was difficult to prevent because of lack of adequate sanitation. Smallpox took hold sometimes, and scurvy was common in outlying French forts, because of the lack of fresh vegetables.

On the subject of food, we have some experiences recorded by one man during a harsh winter in Acadia. The food was dull and meagre, for day after day, a two course meal was served: a bowl of pea soup with a piece of pork dropped in, followed by a ship's-biscuit, halved and toasted. However, the diet of both armies in normal times was generally more varied.

In the forts food could be very plentiful. The following list shows the regular items, which would appear on the menu during a week:

Basic food for French and British: salt pork or beef, bread or hard biscuit.

Additional items:

French: Dried peas, spices, chocolate, cabbages (from a fort garden), and wine or brandy.

British: codfish, oatmeal, beans and peas, rice and fruit, butter and cheese and beer or rum.

With a little resourcefulness many men found they could eat reasonably well. At one fort some men even kept their own cows.

Both British and French soldiers wore uniforms, but there was little chance of getting replacements when the original ones wore out. So do not imagine the British grenadier, for instance, was always as well turned out in his pressed, scarlet tunic, bright belt and gleaming buttons as the next picture shows. The regulars would arrive in America smartly dressed, but with time the equipment would wear out; replacements, even if they could be had, were bought out of the soldier's pay. The main uniform colours were British red and white, and French white and blue; but the exact design and the colour of the many other items (gaiters, mitre-shaped headgear, socks, buckles) were left to the regimental colonels. And in practice, the fit and appearance of the uniform left much to be desired. A British sergeant complained bitterly in one of his letters home that his uniform 'was so tight that to stoop was more than our small clothes were worth—buttons flying, knees bursting, back parts rending'. Lieutenant John Knox wrote an account of life in Acadia, and said that soldiers 'had as grotesque an appearance as a detachment of *irregulars*, occasioned by the length of their beards, the disordered shape of their hats and the raggedness of their party-coloured clothing'. Patching was

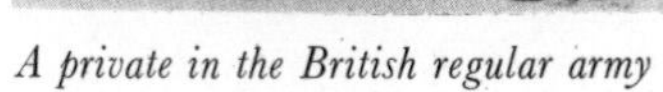

A private in the British regular army

A British officer of the Grenadiers

very common, and the tail of the jacket was used for this purpose. An Indian garment called a 'mitasse' became very fashionable. It was made of coarse woollen cloth, shaped into two tubes and pulled over each leg; as it was loose, it was folded and held in place by gaiters at the knee and ankle.

Such was the dress of the regulars. The colonials were also supposed to be uniformed, but the impression left by some descriptions is of shabby and dirty civilian clothing. Some special regiments had a sort of uniform: George Washington's Virginians wore rifle-shirts (garments looking like dressing-gowns, made of deerskin, belted and reaching below the knee) and green leggings. The French colonials, the Canadians, had

A French-Canadian militiaman

A French regular soldier

'gone native' to an even greater extent than the British. They often dressed exactly as Indians, in moccasins, blankets and paint!

The weapon of the eighteenth century soldier was the flintlock musket. It weighed 12 lb and had a barrel just over three feet long, with a hole (called the bore) of about $\frac{3}{4}$ inch. This musket fired a 'shot', which was usually a lead ball weighing an ounce.

The firing mechanism gave the musket its description as a flintlock. This was the way a spark was produced by 'triggering' or striking a flint against a piece of iron or steel.

(You can see a detailed diagrammatic account on page 64, prepared by Fort Ticonderoga Museum.)

Perhaps you think that this was not very efficient by modern standards. The flintlock had three weaknesses. First, the black powder produced so much smoke that an army quickly became covered in a grey fog. Secondly, real accuracy was judged to be no more than sixty yards, because of what was called 'windage'. (This was the tiny space between ball and barrel, which was necessary because there was always a little powder residue left after the explosion.) Fired wildly, without any particular aim in mind, the musket ball could reach 400 yards. Thirdly, the flint easily wore out: twenty-five shots were about its limit. But they were cheaply made. A flint measured 1 inch by $1\frac{1}{4}$ inch by $\frac{3}{8}$ inch, and armies carried stores of flints running into hundreds of thousands.

Nevertheless the flintlock musket was a practical weapon, and was in regular use by soldiers for well over a century. It probably misfired once in twenty-five shots. There was one serious problem: rain. During a downpour the flintlock was practically useless (do you remember Washington at Great Meadows?). In a mist a soldier was lucky if he fired one shot in three.

In the 1750s a paper cartridge, made up of the lead ball and powder, was used by the soldiers. They had to bite off the end of this cartridge before using, which meant that good front teeth were necessary. You can imagine that some men would deliberately knock out their front teeth to avoid military service!

There was a tremendous variation in the rate of fire between different armies. In the kind of warfare which a man trained in Europe was used to, massed lines of troops would march forward, the front line firing first then kneeling to reload, whilst another line fired over their heads. Obviously this demanded discipline. Aiming and then firing together was given more

How a flintlock musket works

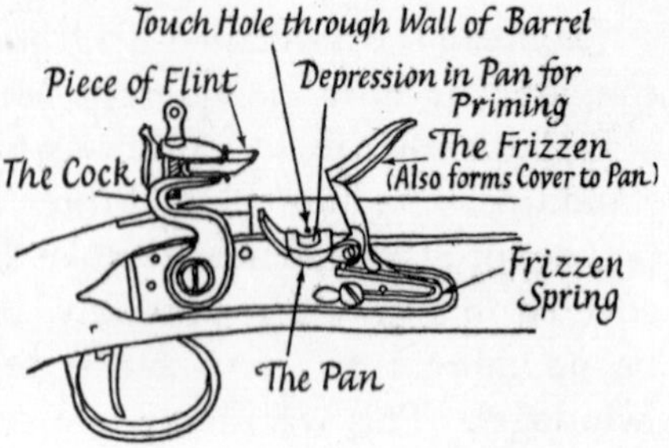

Touch Hole through Wall of Barrel
Piece of Flint
Depression in Pan for Priming
The Frizzen (Also forms Cover to Pan)
The Cock
Frizzen Spring
The Pan

Piece at half cock, frizzen open. You pour a little powder into hollow in pan and snap frizzen shut. Then you pour powder charge into muzzle, drop in the bullet and ram down a light paper wad with the ram rod. A prepared paper cartridge is a paper tube holding ball and powder for priming and load, its paper is used for the wad. The military normally used cartridges, civilians loose powder from a powder horn and a bullet pouch.

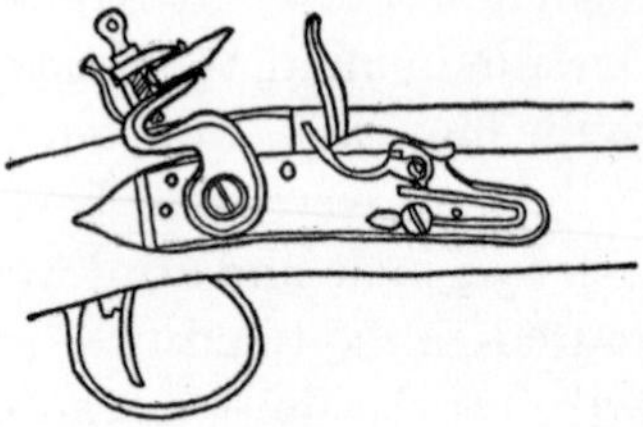

Bring cock back to full cock and you are ready to fire.

You pull the trigger, the flint is knocked smartly against the frizzen making sparks and kicking back the frizzen thus opening pan and exposing priming to sparks. A flint is good for some 20–30 shots before it wears out.

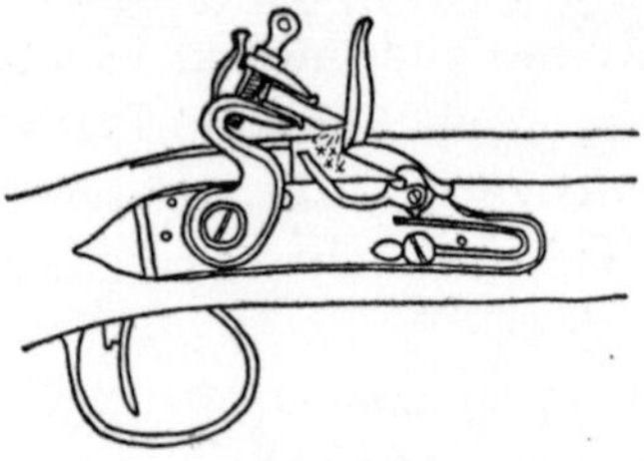

The cock is stopped by a shoulder, the frizzen snaps all the way open. The priming ignites and flashes through the touch hole setting off powder charge in the barrel. There is almost no time lag between pulling trigger and gun going off if gun is properly made and in good condition, perhaps 1/10 to 1/5 second. You now pull cock back to half cock, and you are back where we started in top sketch.

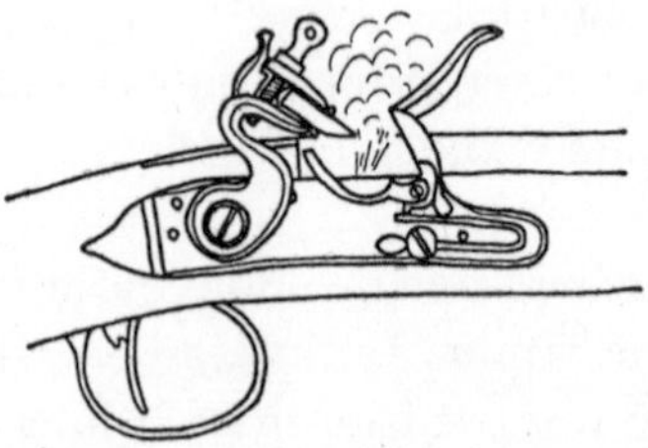

With this military musket you should hit a man almost certainly at 50 yards. Much beyond that it would be a matter of luck, although bullet is effective much farther. You could load and fire 3 to 4 times a minute. The flintlock rifle was much more accurate but not so well suited to general army use.

attention by the British than the French. One of Wolfe's training instructions said, 'There is no necessity of firing very fast; a cool, well-levelled fire is much more destructive and formidable than the quickest fire in confusion.' Well-trained troops could fire, perhaps, three volleys a minute. But marksmanship as an art was not given much attention.

Much of a soldier's life in America consisted of either building or besieging forts. There were several kinds. The easiest to build was the wooden stockade, like that which George Washington erected called Fort Necessity. A cannon could demolish it with ease, as it was only made of twelve-foot logs, stood on end in a deep trench; but remember the forests and mountains made the movement of artillery difficult. An improved fort would use logs and earth in several rows; the great forts of the period, for instance that at Ticonderoga, were like this, and stone 'facing' was added in time. Besieging one of these forts was a major operation. No area of land could be claimed by either the French or the British if an opposing fort in the area remained untaken. Cannon was vital. The best cannons were made of bronze because it did not rust, and they fired over half a mile fairly accurately. They were light to handle, in contrast to the cast iron ones weighing two tons or more that were used inside a fort. (See page 79.)

The rules or conventions of war in those days were such that a commander was expected to defend his fort vigorously until a breach in the walls had been made; then he could surrender without being called a coward, and his men would be treated fairly. If he chose to fight on, and the fort was eventually stormed, the garrison were savagely persecuted.

11 Combined Operations at Louisbourg

Louisbourg was the strongest fortress in French or British North America. It was on a French island off the north coast of Acadia, and it controlled the entrance to the great St Lawrence River. At dawn on 2 June 1758 the horizon beyond the harbour of Louisbourg showed a mass of white sail. Admiral Boscawen and General Amherst had arrived with twenty-three huge *ships-of-the-line*, eighteen *frigates* and a vast fleet of transports carrying nearly 12,000 regular soldiers. The British had come to seize Louisbourg from its French governor, Drucour, and its garrison of 3,500 defenders. The British superiority was very great, but Louisbourg had a fine natural defence in its rocky coastline.

The fleet sailed into Gabarus Bay, and in the afternoon Amherst, his brigadier, James Wolfe, and a number of other officers reconnoitred the shore. The prospect looked hopeless. Over two hundred cannons and mortars mounted on walls and earthworks; four enormous *bastions* along a thousand-yard front around the town; two powerful gun batteries, on Goat Island and on the heights above the town: these made up a ring of fortifications a mile and a half long. On either side the craggy shore stretched for miles, so landings could only be made at a few points; and the French had made sure these points were well guarded. The white foam all along this coast showed clearly the hazards to ships which went too close in-shore. Through the narrow harbour entrance Amherst and Wolfe saw five French ships-of-the-line and seven frigates; their five hundred guns would make a direct harbour attack suicidal.

Despite the risks, a plan was made. West of Louisbourg there were three possible landing points: Freshwater Cove, Flat Point and White Point. In the plan the second and third

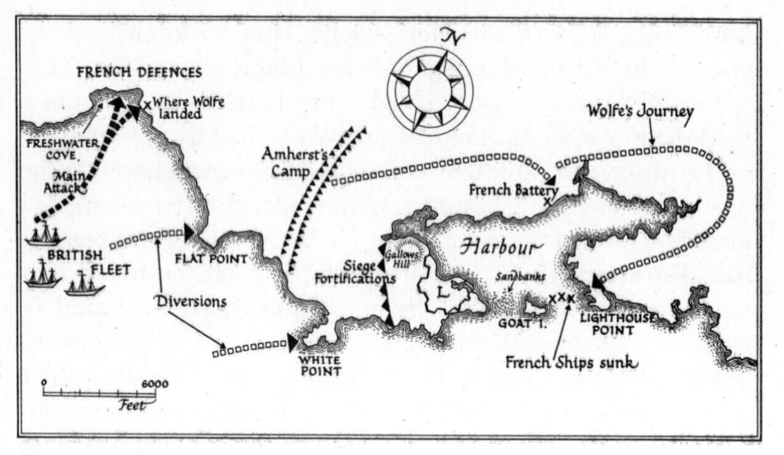

The siege of Louisbourg 1758

were to be threatened by a mock attack, whilst Wolfe's men forced a landing at Freshwater Cove. For days the British fleet waited for good weather. High surf, fog, a gale, more fog and heavy rain followed each other, until on 8 June the seas became calm at last. Wolfe's men made for the shore, which was a crescent-shaped beach about four hundred yards long. Wolfe did not know that a thousand hidden Frenchmen watched his approach. The French allowed the enemy to come in close before opening fire; then grapeshot raked the open boats. It quickly became clear that a landing was impossible without huge casualties, so Wolfe signalled the boats to veer aside, before turning back. But to the right, three boats were caught by the swift undercurrent and carried round a small headland. They were swept onto a narrow, rocky beach which was hidden from the open sea and at least half a mile from the main French positions. Wolfe saw what was happening, and instantly directed the boats near him to follow.

It was a hazardous affair. Many boats had their bottoms ripped open on hidden rocks, and their occupants were dragged about in the surf; from the first three boats, only a dozen men reached the shore safely. They scrambled up the crags to find themselves against fifty Frenchmen and Indians —five of the dozen were killed immediately. But the others held their ground until relief came. Wolfe had by now arrived, and with several hundred soldiers led a bayonet charge to the nearest French gun battery. Meanwhile, the rest of Wolfe's force had landed on the main beach, because these happenings had distracted the French attention. The French found that they were being attacked from left and right; so, afraid of being cut off from Louisbourg itself they fled to the woods. They were soon joined by their comrades from the other coastal defences as far as White Point. Round one in the contest had gone to the British, for they now had a good stretch of coast under their control. But Wolfe said afterwards, 'We made a rash and ill-advised attempt to land, and by the greatest good fortune imaginable, we succeeded.'

Louisbourg still stood unconquered. Amherst had brought a great deal of siege equipment with his army, and he now set about the elaborate preparations needed. Day after day the ships brought guns and stores to Flat Point Cove. The waves made things difficult: a hundred boats were lost on submerged rocks in the first few days. It was not until ten days later that the big siege guns were brought ashore. The British began trench digging about half a mile from Louisbourg's ramparts —just out of cannon shot. Wolfe with a detachment of soldiers was sent round the back of the town to silence the outpost batteries. He took Lighthouse Point and bombarded Goat Island's defences into submission. Admiral Boscawen now had a good chance of forcing a passage with his fleet into the main harbour. But the French had not been idle. Louisbourg's commander, Drucour, saw the danger, and on a dark, foggy night four large ships were towed to the entrance and sunk.

Meanwhile, Wolfe had returned to the main body of Amherst's army, which was gradually edging forward. The digging of trenches was a long job and it was not until the evening of 16 July that Wolfe was able to seize a small ridge, called Gallows Hill, only three hundred yards from the northern bastion of Louisbourg. His small force was pelted with grapeshot, but, once there, it could not be removed. It was obvious that the end would not be long.

You must not think of the French and British forces at Louisbourg as enemies to the point of bitterness. There were many small incidents—courtesies they might be called—between the two sides. Flags of truce were common in long sieges, mainly for the moving of wounded. The French governor on one occasion offered his surgeon, a man of high distinction, to any English officer who should need his services. Letters were exchanged between captured wounded and their own sides. Amherst sent Madame Drucour, the governor's wife, a gift of West Indian pineapples, with a note expressing his 'regret at the disquiet' under which she was suffering. On yet another occasion, the war stood still whilst an English officer's wife visited a distant cousin in the French garrison!

The end came swiftly. On 21 July 1758 a lucky shell struck a powder store on a French ship in the harbour; a fire was started that could not be put out, and the flames spread to two others. On shore the masonry of the bastions was crumbling under gunfire. A quarter of the French garrison were in hospital. Drucour realised he could not expect a relief force, and he felt he had done his duty as he saw it: to keep going until it was so late in the season that the British would not be able to move on Quebec. On 26 July he asked for terms. The British demanded unconditional surrender. Drucour hesitated at such a humiliation, and he wrote out a refusal which was sent immediately by messenger. One of his advisers protested vigorously:

> 'For the good of the State, the preservation of the King's subjects and averting the horrors shocking to humanity, I

am obliged to lay before your eyes the consequences that may ensue. What will become of the 4,000 souls who compose the families of this town, of the thousand sick in hospitals and the officers and crews of our unfortunate ships? They will be delivered over to *carnage* and the rage of an *unbridled* soldiery, eager for plunder. Thus they will all be destroyed, and the memory of their fate will live forever in our colonies.'

This shows you clearly one of the traditions of siege warfare: that a refusal of terms will result in a town being plundered (or 'sacked' as it is called). Drucour gave way. A man was sent quickly to change Drucour's note into one of acceptance. An Englishman in Wolfe's camp saw what happened: 'A lieutenant-colonel came running out of the garrison, making signs at a distance, and bawling out as loud as he could, "We accept, We accept."'

General Amherst (centre) directing the siege of Louisbourg

So ended the siege of Louisbourg. The French had made a gallant effort, but the odds were too great. Celebrations and sermons of thanksgiving spread throughout the English colonies as the news reached them. For one Englishman, however, the capture of Louisbourg was not enough:

> 'We are gathering strawberries and other wild fruits of the country, with a seeming indifference about what is doing in other parts of the world. This damned French garrison takes up our time and attention, which might be better bestowed. I cannot look coolly upon the bloody inroads of those hell-hounds, the Canadians, and if nothing further is to be done, I must desire leave to quit the army.'

This Englishman did not, of course, quit the army. Next year, he sailed for Quebec and died there. His name was James Wolfe.

The second expedition of 1758, the one to take Fort Duquesne, proved to have an easy task. Careful preparations were made by a very capable man, Forbes, for the fate of Braddock back in '55 was still in everyone's mind. But other small attacks which had been made on the long line of French communications, from Duquesne back to Montreal, had been very successful. The French became alarmed at their exposed position, so they blew up Fort Duquesne and disappeared before Forbes even arrived.

The third expedition of 1758 was a different matter altogether.

12 Ticonderoga: Montcalm's Great Victory

'Ticonderoga' is an American Indian word meaning, 'at the junction of two waterways'. The third major British onslaught of 1758 was intended to capture this French fort situated where the waters of Lake George and Lake Champlain meet. The fort had been started in 1755, when the French governor at Quebec decided to strengthen his hold on the Lake Champlain area. The French called it Fort Carillon, although it is now better known by the Indian name, which the British gave it later on: Ticonderoga. If you look at the plan of the region on page 67, you will notice its position on a narrow headland. There is an aerial photograph below, which shows

Fort Ticonderoga (below centre) as it is today. The landscape is much as it was in 1758. Lake George lies in the background beyond the woods

you the accurate reconstruction of the fort, as it is today. There is very little difference in the countryside around Ticonderoga between today and the 1750s, except that the area close to the fort itself was then clear of trees. Lake George is in the background, and you will see how densely wooded the land was.

The fort is four-sided with pointed spurs, called bastions, jutting out from its four corners. These bastions allowed the defenders to deliver flanking fire. The fort is further guarded by two outworks called *demi-lunes*, one to the north, the other to the west. In 1755 the French first built the walls of great, squared timber, laid horizontally and filled behind with earth. This could easily be repaired, but the wood soon rotted, so some stone facings were added in the next year.

To capture this powerful fort, Pitt appointed as Commander-in-Chief James Abercrombie. He was not a good choice: he suffered from bad health and was regarded as being over-cautious. The local colonial troops called him, 'Mrs Nabbycromby'. However, Pitt put a brilliant officer under him. His name was Lord Howe; only thirty-three years old, he was already a first-rate combat leader, and possibly a real rival to Montcalm. Unlike Braddock before him, he really tried to train the British regular soldier to fight in the forest and to use the forest as an ally, not see it as an enemy. But his death, early on, was a disaster for the expedition.

At Ticonderoga Montcalm had 3,500 men. He had plenty of warning of Abercrombie's approach from the south, and he set to work on the construction of an outer defence, half a mile from the fort. Across a narrow ridge an enormous wall of logs was made. Records show that logs were laid two or three deep, and some individual logs were three feet in diameter! All Montcalm's force worked hard on the task for two days. What chance had an attacker of getting through? If he used artillery, a very good one; we shall see that everything depended on this fact.

Early in July 1758 Abercrombie supervised the launching of a great fleet of 900 boats on the southern shores of Lake George. On board were enough soldiers to outnumber the French by three to one. This force rowed northwards, and landed at a point where the lake narrows before flowing into Lake Champlain. There was, of course, a small French outpost here, but its guards quickly withdrew. Abercrombie had chosen the western side of the lake to land, obviously thinking

Courtesy: Glens Falls Insurance Company, Glens Falls, New York

General Abercrombie watching his expedition set out from the shores of Lake George for Ticonderoga

that, although it was the long way round, he would at least be on the same bank as Ticonderoga. Traders normally used a portage track between the two lakes (you can see it marked on the sketch-map on page 76), but Abercrombie seems to have forgotten this.

Can you imagine the task of moving 10,000 troops through dense, trackless forest without maps? Lord Howe took some men forward, and soon found it was impossible. But just as he was about to turn back, he accidentally met the rearguard of the French force, which was withdrawing to the fort. Some shots were fired, and Howe, at the head of his men was instantly killed. Chaos followed: some men pressed on, some returned. Order was not restored until nightfall, and if the French had sent out some Indians, there would have been a massacre. But Montcalm had only sixteen Indians in his entire army.

Abercrombie was able to regroup his army back at the landing place. An officer reminded him of the traders' track, and he decided to try this. He met no resistance on the two crossings, even at the sawmill. Perhaps this made him overconfident, and he saw the chances of a great British victory were good. Then two disastrous decisions were taken. First, a young engineer was asked for his opinion of the defences; he replied that a frontal attack would easily overwhelm them. Secondly, Abercrombie, who had left his heavy cannon on the boats, decided not to bother about them.

If you think carefully about the situation, you will see that there were three things Abercrombie could have done:

1. Lay siege, and force the garrison to surrender. This was a sound idea, because the French force at Ticonderoga was a large one compared with the size of the fort, and probably there was only a few days' food supply (records have been found to show that in fact it was five days).
2. Bombard the wall and the fort. Soldiers who were there felt that a day's artillery preparation and 10,000 men should easily have taken the fort.
3. Launch an immediate infantry attack.

Perhaps Abercrombie feared the French would send reinforcements across Lake Champlain, but in choosing the third alternative he was certainly taking the worst of the choices. A military expert has said, 'Abercrombie must have lost his wits that day.'

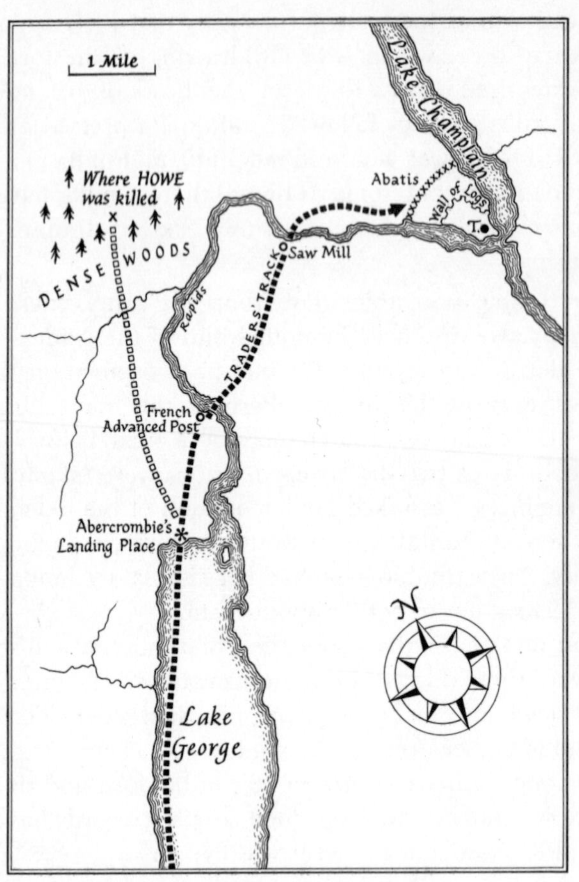

Abercrombie's assault on Fort Ticonderoga 1758

He ordered the infantry to make an attack, straight at the French defences. But there was more to overcome than just a wall of logs. For the French had cleared a big open area in front of the wall, and stretched an *abatis* right across it made of tree tops piled high. It was also more than just a man-made hedge, for the branches had been sharpened, then hidden by leaves; it proved a most effective early form of barbed wire!

There are many accounts of the murderous clash which

followed. A Frenchman described the opening of the biggest battle ever fought, to that date, anywhere in North America: 'At half past twelve the English army *debouched* upon us'. Abercrombie had given orders that the log ramparts were to be 'carried with the bayonet', but the French musket fire was too strong. A crash of exploding firearms split the air, and grapeshot and musket balls swept the whole English line. By mid-afternoon, under a scorching July sun:

> 'The scene was frightful. Masses of infuriated men who could not go forward and would not go back; straining for an enemy they could not reach, and firing on an enemy they could not see; caught in the entanglement of fallen trees; tripped by briars, stumbling over logs, tearing through boughs; shouting, yelling, cursing, and pelted all the time with bullets that killed them by scores, stretched them on the ground, or hung them on jagged branches in strange attitudes of death.'

An English lieutenant, John Knox, was there. He said, 'I wish I could throw a veil over what is to follow: I am at a loss how to proceed. I believe we were one and all *infatuated* with the notion of carrying every obstacle.' By seven in the evening the British had launched six direct assaults on the French defences. The last one, by the 42nd Highlanders (the famous Black Watch Regiment), cost five hundred casualties alone. The gallantry was great, but useless.

Abercrombie at last retreated, leaving over 1,600 killed, wounded or missing. The French had lost hardly a quarter of that number. Abercrombie's withdrawal was final. Even the French were surprised that he did not return next day. Looking back you might wonder why, for he still had the most overwhelming odds in his favour. The disasters of that July day may have unnerved him; no one will ever know the real reason. Anyway, he was quietly removed from his position as Commander-in-Chief.

Montcalm being hailed after his victory at Ticonderoga in 1758

1759: The Anti-climax

In 1759 William Pitt issued the following clear instructions to the new C.-in-C. British Forces, North America, General Amherst. He was to move against Ticonderoga and Crown Point, and then on to Canada. At the same time James Wolfe was to seize Quebec, and move up the St Lawrence. The two men were to meet at Montreal.

Remember the Amherst we saw at Louisbourg? He was efficient and painstaking. As he marched north from New York, intent on recovering British honour before Ticonderoga, he was equally painstaking. He had with him a report of the fort's defences which a scouting party had made early in the year. This report showed important differences between the task he faced and that in which Abercrombie had failed so badly. Now, only five hundred defended the fort; food was short and scurvy had killed forty men already. Also, Amherst made it clear to his men that he was not going to repeat the artillery mistake again.

However, unknown to the British, the French had made a decision. They were being attacked at so many points all over the area that they would have to concentrate their smaller numbers around Montreal and Quebec. Montcalm had already left for Quebec, and preparations for the evacuation of Ticonderoga were being made. So, as the British were slowly hauling their heavy cannon into place, the French commander and his few hundred troops slipped away. But one Frenchman deserted, and took news of a lighted fuse in the central powder magazine to Amherst. Amherst offered a hundred guineas (worth nearly £1,000 today) to anyone brave or perhaps foolhardy enough to go and put it out. No one took up the offer, and one hour before midnight the central part of Ticonderoga exploded in a brilliant flash, and burned for a week. Amherst's campaign had taken an empty, shattered fort, at the cost of sixteen killed. The great '59 assault had fizzled out. The final fall of Canada had to wait until 1760.

One of the original cannons now standing on the ramparts of the restored Fort Ticonderoga

13 Wolfe Lays Siege to Quebec

'Damn me, if there are not a thousand places in the Thames fifty times more hazardous than this; I am ashamed that Englishmen should make such a *rout* about it.' Old Tom Killick, Master of the 'Goodwill', was expressing his thoughts after passing the difficult Traverse on the great River St Lawrence. He was one of the many skippers of old transports, who mocked at the precautions taken by the senior officers of the main fleet; for Killick piloted his ship merely by the look of the water, and by shouting orders with a trumpet in hand from the captain's bridge. Such methods hardly suited the fleet's C.-in-C., Admiral Saunders. Three days detailed inspection of the treacherous sandbanks were needed before his navigator, James Cook, was 'satisfied with being acquainted with ye Channel.' (Mr Cook was learning the trade that later took him to Australia and the South Seas.)

It was a magnificent piece of navigation. In June 1759, with no loss, a formidable battle fleet of forty-nine sail and 120 transports went up the St Lawrence. It took just five weeks to reach the Island of Orleans, very near Quebec, from Louisbourg. Fogs, difficult winds and unknown sandbanks had all been successfully overcome.

The fleet anchored off the south shore of the island. Lieutenant Knox was there and has given us an account of what the scene looked like:

> 'Delightful country on every side; windmills, watermills, churches, chapels and compact farmhouses all built with stone. The lands appear to be everywhere well cultivated, and with the help of my glass I can discern that they are sowed with flax, wheat, barley, peas etc.'

The army landed, and found there were no fortifications on the island; but they did find a letter in one of the churches. It was addressed to 'The Worthy Officers of the British Army', and the French priest who wrote it said he wished they had come sooner, so that they could have enjoyed the asparagus and radishes which had now, he feared, gone to seed. Knox says the British officers were not very amused at the 'frothy politeness' of their enemy, the French!

In command of this expedition to seize Quebec was James Wolfe, now promoted to the rank of General. He immediately left the army camp, and with a small escort pushed quickly through some woods to the western tip of the island—eager to see the fortress he had come so far to attack. The city of Quebec, three miles distant, faced him across the waters of the St Lawrence. It stood perched high on a point of land between the great river and its tributary, the St Charles River. Wolfe could easily make out the two parts of the city: a cluster of houses which made up the Lower Town; and more houses, the cathedral and convent spires and trees in the large gardens of the Upper Town, which he could guess was about 200 feet above the river. Just to the left of the city he saw the great, rocky, 350-foot-high mass of land called Cape Diamond. Everywhere gun batteries were obvious, and Wolfe knew it would be suicidal to attack up those cliffs. He was not very happy either with the clear view he had of the Beauport Shore, just across the channel from him on the north bank. His eye moved from the city walls, across the St Charles, past broad flats of mud, across the estuary of another small river, along great military earthworks which the French had built, until it came to rest on the beautiful and hazardous waterfalls at Montmorency: in all, a six-mile collection of military camps, *redoubts* and gun batteries. To the other side of Quebec, he could look from where he stood straight up the St Lawrence. He could not quite see what the coast was like because it curved away slightly behind Cape Diamond, but he could imagine it would be very steep and well wooded.

Quebec, from Point Levis. (See maps on pages 84 and 91).

Meanwhile, Saunders was concerned for the safety of his fleet, because the first anchorage proved unsatisfactory. In the first two days the ships rode out a storm and faced a fireship attack. A second fireship onslaught was made at midnight on 28 June: seven slow-moving hulks were seen drifting from Quebec, but the French seem to have lost their nerve, and they fired them too early—half a mile away in fact. This gave ample warning: 'Certainly the grandest fireworks that can be possibly conceived', wrote an Englishman in his diary. As the flaming ships drifted alongside a British vessel, they were edged away with grappling irons and boathooks, so that the current could carry them to the shore.

By July a camp had been established on the Island of Orleans, and a secure anchorage found. But the following weeks were full of frustration. Point Levis, opposite Quebec on the south shore, was taken by Wolfe's men, and a bombardment begun of the Quebec defences. This barrage went on, at intervals, for six weeks, but it became obvious that no final decision was going to be reached this way. So Wolfe turned his forces to the Montmorency region. The spectacular waterfalls there were scaled, but attacks on the heavily fortified Beauport area were easily beaten off by the French. For example, in two disastrous minutes on 31 July, four hundred men of the Louisbourg Grenadiers fell to their deaths down a cliffside at Montmorency which they had been vainly attacking.

Throughout August tempers were becoming frayed. Indian allies of the French began scalping English sentries in isolated outposts, so Wolfe ordered his soldiers to retaliate: many of the small French settlements stretching eastwards along the banks of the St Lawrence were razed to the ground. Then the City of Quebec was given a severe bombardment. On one day the Lower Town caught fire at one o'clock in the morning and burned furiously until ten; it was nearly destroyed, with 152 houses reduced to ashes. This was an unpleasant part of the story. A Frenchman's diary records his view that, 'Wolfe's prime target was the people of Quebec.' Wolfe was not exactly breaking the laws of war, but it seems clear that the gunfire was no longer directed at mainly military targets.

Wolfe's difficulties can be seen if we look at the problem of *strategy*. The British faced a fortress on top of a cliff: frontal attack would be disastrous. Therefore, Quebec must be attacked round its flanks. To a British soldier, an assault up-river (i.e. on the left flank) looked impossible. How could a fleet get through the Quebec Narrows (1,300 yards wide), with its fierce ebb tide, a prevailing west wind and the many guns on the cliffs above. Yet attempts to seize Quebec from below the city (i.e. on the right flank) had already proved costly in men and time. Two rivers, the Beauport mud flats and strong French gun batteries protected this area.

Wolfe felt he was being taught a bitter lesson, and his early hopes were fast fading. The strain on his health was beginning

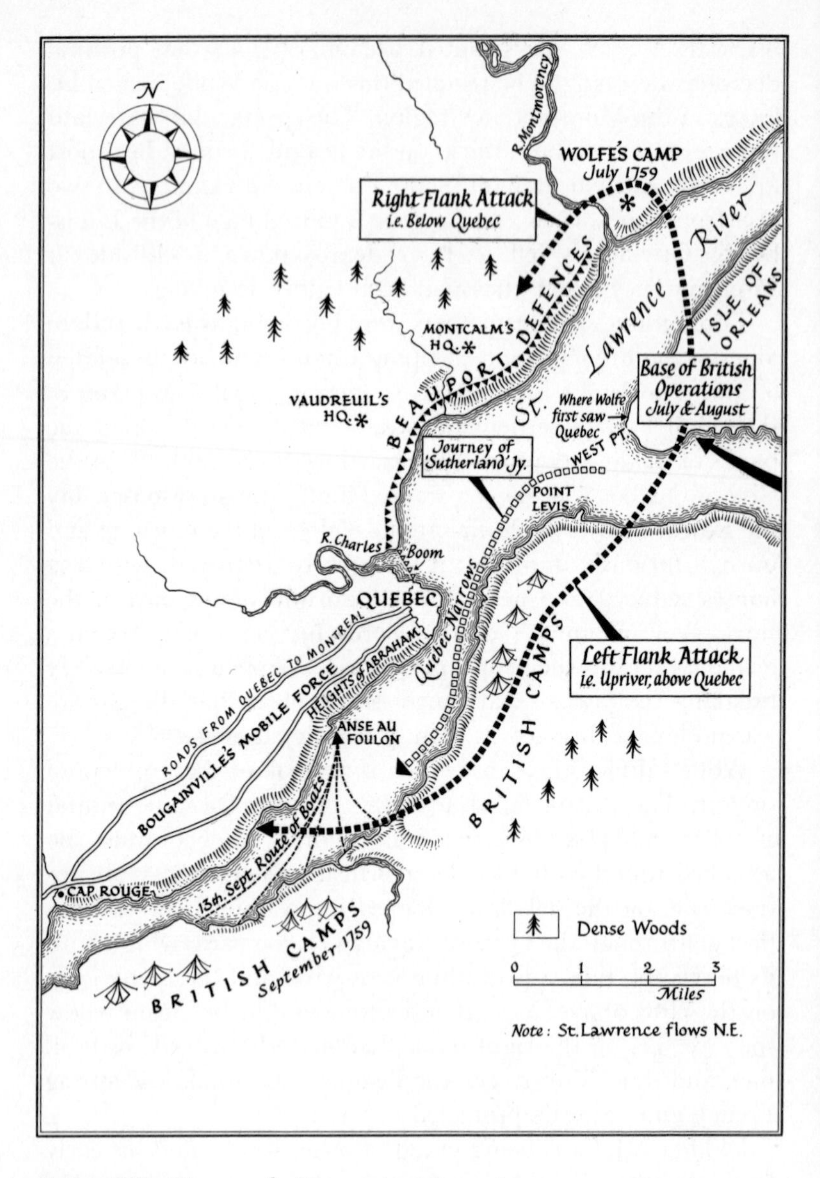

Quebec 1759: The area of military and naval operations

to show: in August he became ill, and was so feverish that he took to his bed for many days. Also in early August, his senior officers had begun to lose confidence in him. They said Wolfe was dithering, and, as Field Marshal Montgomery has said about his own experiences in the Second World War, 'Indecision and hesitation are fatal in any officer; in a C.-in-C. they are criminal.' Wolfe's qualities of determination and resolution were never more needed than in that late summer of 1759.

The crisis was at hand. Two decisions had been taken which were now to prove most important. First, on 17 July, Saunders had ordered the big fifty-gun ship, 'Sutherland', 'to pass up beyond Quebec at the first fair wind'. This was done at dusk on the following evening. The captain's report of steep, wooded cliffs did not give Wolfe much comfort; but, it proved the navy could do what the army had thought impossible. Secondly, on 27 August, Wolfe called for suggestions from his senior officers. They wrote: 'The most probable method of striking an effectual blow is to bring the troops to the south shore, and to direct operations above the Town.' This meant that a determined attack on Quebec could be attempted on the left flank. Wolfe ordered the evacuation of his forces from the Montmorency region, in preparation for such an attempt.

In the French camp, the Governor of New France, Vaudreuil, noted the British withdrawal with great pleasure. He said: 'Everything proves the grand design of the English has failed.'

14 Battle is Joined: the Heights of Abraham

The Marquis de Montcalm had good reason to feel that the way he was defending Quebec was the right one. He had refused to be drawn into open battle, because he knew the British had superiority in numbers. He let Wolfe wear his men out in their attacks on the powerful French defences of the Beauport shore and at Montmorency. Montcalm had a good line of communication for supplies and food running westwards out of Quebec to Montreal, so he could afford to wait. Wolfe could not—he dare not wait till the St Lawrence froze.

The French had no real fear either of an attack from above the city. They had not been idle. As soon as the 'Sutherland' showed it could sail through the Quebec Narrows, Montcalm had sent Colonel Bougainville to a place called Cap Rouge. It was seven miles up-river from Quebec on the north shore, where a British landing would be easy. With Bougainville, one of France's most promising soldiers, went a highly trained, mobile force of perhaps the finest thousand men in Montcalm's army.

Also, at strategic points along the cliff top between Quebec and Cap Rouge, guards were placed. They were mostly in groups of fifty, although at one point, the Anse au Foulon, a hundred men were posted. The Anse au Foulon today is called Wolfe's Cove. It has cliffs rising 175 feet above the St Lawrence. The cove was formed by a stream which cut a small notch in the cliffs; a steep path, wide enough for two men, ran upwards across the face of this cliff. (This way up is still there today, although later generations have changed the path into a very steep motor road.)

Meanwhile Wolfe was going ahead with his preparations,

and by the second week in September most of the British army was camped on the south shore of the St Lawrence, opposite Quebec. Wolfe was fully aware that Bougainville's men could move swiftly to meet any British troops attempting to land in large numbers on the north shore. The senior British officers favoured fighting it out with Bougainville at Cap Rouge, but Wolfe had other ideas. He made his own decision: a secret night landing would be made at the Anse au Foulon. It was a courageous, if rash, decision, for Montcalm had said: 'A hundred men there could stop an army.'

Wolfe had luck on his side. The French commander at the top of the cliff was Duchambon de Vergor. Do you remember him? He was the man who, four years before, had surrendered Fort Beauséjour to the English in such suspicious and cowardly circumstances. It was perhaps unfortunate for the French that the immediate responsibility for stopping Wolfe was to rest on this man's shoulders.

As night fell on 12 September, 1,800 men settled into thirty large, flat-bottomed rowboats, drawn up on the south shore. These men were to be the advance force. They were to be

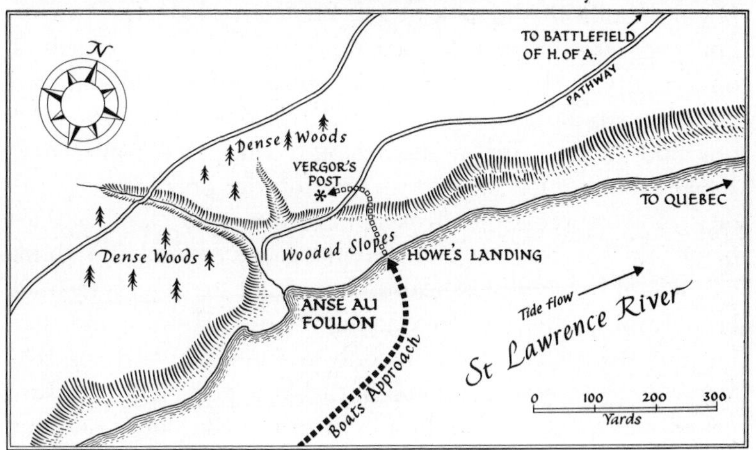

The Anse au Foulon

followed by armed vessels with stores and ammunition, and other ships full of troops. Wolfe wanted at least 4,000 men at the top of the cliff by the early morning. At 2 a.m. the boats cast off. A diary of one of the men records: 'Fine weather, night calm, silence over all.' No man was allowed to speak, and even the rowlocks were muffled with felt. The moon had risen, but was in the last quarter, so not likely to reveal much of what was going on.

There are many legends of those famous hours. The best known tells of Wolfe reciting a verse from the poem, 'Elegy in a Country Churchyard', with its well-known line, 'The paths of glory lead but to the grave'. There does not seem to be much truth in this story. Wolfe may have said it a day or so before, but can you imagine the C.-in-C. talking whilst all the men had been ordered into silence!

In the last half hour of darkness, and after many miles of rowing and drifting with the tide, the leading boat grated on the gravel under the dark cliffs. In it were twenty-four volunteers of Colonel Howe's Light Infantry. They were challenged by a French sentry further along the beach: 'Qui vive?'; a Highland officer who spoke fluent French replied: 'La France', and they were allowed to pass. There was a tense moment of uncertainty as they tried to make out just where the path up the Anse au Foulon was; it was still very dark, and they could not find it. So, after a hurried and whispered conference, Howe took his men straight up the cliffside. There was a great deal of loose rock and broken tree stumps to clamber over before the top was reached. Should you try it today, I think you would be left with a healthy respect for the achievement of Howe and his men. (When daylight came, Howe found that he had missed the path by only a hundred yards or so.) Vergor's small post at the top of the Anse au Foulon was surprised and quickly taken by the British. Some stories say that Vergor was in bed when Howe arrived, and others say he had given sixty of his hundred men leave to work in the hayfields! Such tales may or may not be true.

The immediate crisis for Wolfe was over, and while the extremely well-organised ferry service by the navy was going on behind, the British army rapidly marshalled itself at the top of the cliffs, and spread out onto the Heights of Abraham. These heights lay not far from the city walls of Quebec, and across them ran the vital French roads of communication to Montreal.

The Landing at the Anse au Foulon

What was Montcalm doing? He had been very effectively persuaded that a new landing was being attempted near Montmorency; the British fleet had sent some of its big ships to make as much noise and clamour as possible in the stretch of water between the Island of Orleans and the Beauport shore. So Montcalm kept the main body of his army in that region and on the alert. As dawn broke, news of a British landing at the Anse au Foulon was brought to him by a badly frightened Canadian. Montcalm hesitated: where was the main assault going to be? Part of the French trouble was an inefficient communication system. Letters had a habit of going astray; rumours would cause even more confusion. Certainly, Montcalm did not know that by now most of the British army was on the Heights of Abraham. He decided to launch an immediate attack on what he must have thought was only a small British force; later he would realise his mistake. He should, of course, have waited for Bougainville and his 1,000 experienced men, who had been sent for. Instead, Montcalm mounted his horse, gave orders for the main French army to follow him, and rode into battle.

This was exactly what Wolfe wanted. All along, through those dreadful months of July and August, he had been out-generalled by Montcalm, who had refused to be drawn into a major battle. Now the tables were turned. Montcalm probably felt he must chance a desperate stroke on the field of battle against an army which he feared was much better than his own.

At six o'clock in the morning, on 13 September 1759, Wolfe saw that most of his troops had disembarked. It takes even a disciplined army many hours to get into battle formation: the British were ready first, but Wolfe waited. He had the utmost confidence in his men, and he knew he had to bring a big French force into battle before he could hope for a decisive victory. When the British line was formed he ordered them to lie down and rest. There were 4,440 of them—all that Wolfe could hope to get up the Anse au Foulon in time—and by lying down, they prevented Montcalm from getting an accurate idea of their numbers. You must not think all was quiet. The British had another reason for lying down, because, erect, they presented easy targets for the French and Indian sharpshooters who were gathering on the flanks. Fierce and bloody skirmishes continued for over an hour before the main battle, while 'the general', said one soldier, 'moved about everywhere'.

There is no accurate record of the exact numbers of French on the field of battle, but it seems likely that the two opposing armies were very similar in strength. The difference lay in quality: Wolfe's men were all highly trained regulars; Montcalm had many colonial troops who had never been drilled in formal battle order.

At five past ten the French moved. They presented a gallant sight as the white and blue uniformed men advanced at a rush

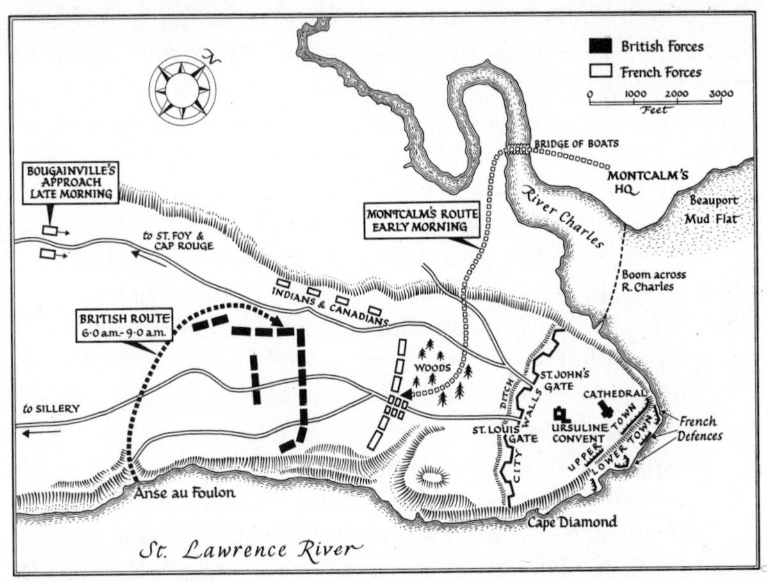

The Battle of the Heights of Abraham, 10 a.m. 13 September 1759

with the ensigns' large silk flags flowing behind them. But they came too quickly. 'We had not gone twenty paces', said a French soldier afterwards, 'when the left was too far to the rear, and the centre too far to the front.' Also they began firing at about 130 yards from the British—far too early—and many threw themselves on the ground to reload, instead of kneeling. (Can you imagine trying to reload a musket through the muzzle while lying down?) These things completely disrupted the French line. The British, who were now standing in line, remained motionless and silent. Wolfe had given a strict order: it said, 'Not to fire a shot until the enemy should be within forty yards of the point of our bayonets'. This took a great deal of courage, with thousands of Frenchmen, firing all the time, getting closer every second. But Wolfe's order was obeyed. There was no way, of course, of giving a single command to everyone, as the noise was tremendous and the British line nearly half a mile wide, but the centre of this line fired simultaneously. The *Brown Bess* musket blew Montcalm's army to ruin, for, says a British army historian, 'it was the most perfect volley ever fired on a battlefield'. The effect was shattering. When the smoke cleared the French line had broken completely; men everywhere were fleeing. So ended one of the great decisive battles of history. It had lasted only ten minutes.

Both commanders were killed. Wolfe died very quickly on the battlefield after being hit twice—once in the wrist, once in the lung—by musket shot. John Knox has given us a clear account of Wolfe's last minutes:

> 'He desired those who were about him to lay him down; being asked if he would have a surgeon, he replied, "It is needless; it is all over with me". One of them then cried out, "They run, see how they run." "Who runs?" demanded our hero, with great earnestness, like a person roused from sleep. The officer answered: "The enemy, Sir; Egad, they give way everywhere." '

Wolfe then talked a moment of the chances of cutting off the enemy's retreat. Knox goes on: 'Then, turning on his side, he added, "Now, God be praised, I will die in peace": and thus expired.'

Montcalm too was wounded. He had been hit in the thigh and stomach and he needed three soldiers to hold him in the saddle as he rode back into Quebec. He died the next day.

Many of the Frenchmen who fled from the battlefield

escaped into the woods and later joined Bougainville, who had arrived too late to do anything. They withdrew westwards to Montreal. Governor Vaudreuil decided to abandon Quebec, and he also made his way to Montreal. He put all the blame for failure on Montcalm. A senior French officer of the regular army was furious at all this: he thought the French should have reformed and attacked again, and he was bitter at Vaudreuil's vicious attack on the dead Montcalm; he was also disgusted at the withdrawal. He said: 'It was not a retreat, but an abominable flight.' The few soldiers left in Quebec surrendered to Wolfe's army, now commanded by Brigadier Murray, on 18 September 1759.

A modern aerial view of the Heights of Abraham. The Anse au Foulon and the old city walls are just off the picture to the left and right respectively

15 The British Keep Quebec in 1760—but only just

Quebec was in a mess. John Knox spent the winter of 1759–60 there, and has told us of the hard work needed to get the place re-fortified and habitable. Two vital questions would be answered in the spring of 1760. Would the French army which had retreated to Montreal after the Battle of the Heights of Abraham come back? Would the French navy get up to Quebec before the British fleet returned when the thaw came?

You might wonder what Quebec was like for the conquerors and conquered in that winter. Good relations were soon established, and Brigadier Murray, Wolfe's successor, stayed on as governor. The British soldiers went to help get the harvest in during the last weeks of September; the Catholic nuns of the city convents knitted long woollen socks for the Scots' Highland Regiment. (One story says the nuns did this because they were so shocked at the sight of the Highlanders' hairy legs below their kilts!) The walls needed a lot of repair work; wood had to be cut for the long winter months. As the weather became colder, the uniform regulations were overlooked when the soldiers added all sorts of thick clothing to their bodies. Knox described some men in the dress of the 'frozen Laplander', and told of squads of soldiers sitting on their behinds and 'tobogganing down from the Upper to the Lower Town'. Then the dreaded scurvy, which had struck Ticonderoga in 1758, struck Quebec late in 1759. Grizzly tales of seven hundred British bodies piled high in the snowdrifts waiting for burial tell just how bad things were.

Meanwhile the French at Montreal prepared to return. They had a good plan: Bougainville was to hold the western and southern routes to the town of Montreal against Amherst coming up from Lake Champlain; another French commander, Levis, was to return to Quebec to reverse the battle of 1759. Levis had 7,000 men who marched along the St Lawrence shore road to Quebec in April 1760; some vessels on the river carried their supplies.

The British were in a difficult position. Murray counted his troops on hearing of the French approach: 3,866 were healthy;

Sir James Murray

2,300 were severely ill. He was not at all happy at the thought of a second battle being fought on the Heights of Abraham, but he had no option. He ordered the able soldiers into formation, and waited patiently for the French assault with some well-placed artillery. Levis launched a powerful attack, but the cannon fire from the British lines was too great, and the French withdrew a little way. Murray decided to give chase and seize the advantage. The Heights of Abraham is a small plateau, and as the British moved forward the high ground was soon left behind. Drifts of unmelted snow made orderly movement impossible; worse still, the cannon on which Murray was relying became completely bogged down. Suddenly out of the woods on the British right flank the French appeared, and although at times soldiers were knee deep in mud, a bitter struggle took place, which lasted all morning. Murray felt afraid of being cut off from Quebec itself, and ordered a retreat. His force scrambled back to the safety of the walled town, but many cannon had to be left behind and 1,100 casualties had been suffered. Levis's army was not strong enough to take the fortress by storm, so a siege was inevitable.

Both sides waited, knowing the fate of Quebec would be decided by the colour of the flag on the first ship to make the five-week journey up the St Lawrence, now the ice had broken. Murray was running short of food, and he knew that if it was the white flag of the Bourbon kings of France, he would have to surrender.

Unknown to both commanders, out in the Atlantic a vital struggle for control of the sea had been taking place. The French government in Paris now had second thoughts about leaving New France to its fate: French ships with supplies and men fought hard to get away from the powerful blockade of the British fleet. They fought in vain. The British navy kept command of the sea.

On 9 May 1760 a frigate anchored off Quebec. This fast-moving ship brought news of the arrival quite soon of the main fleet. At the mast-head was a British flag. Levis and his men, their spirits low, returned to Montreal. They knew the fate of New France was sealed.

The final act is quickly told. In the next month Amherst and Murray closed the ring around Montreal, and on 8 September 1760 Governor Vaudreuil surrendered New France to British control. In 1763 the British and French ended their fighting in Europe, and by the peace treaty Canada became part of the British Empire. The French settlers did not leave, and in the years to come . . . But that is part of another story.

16 Why did the British Win?

You have now read the story of *how* the struggle for Canada ended in Britain's favour. Perhaps you would like to ask yourself the question: why did the British win? Remember the original contest was centred in the Ohio valley, where the French were threatening to cut the British colonists' route westwards. We have seen how Pitt saw the solution to the problem with masterly directness: conquer French Canada, and the Ohio French would be isolated. And to Pitt's way of thinking it followed that if British naval power could cut Canadian communications with France, then New France would be isolated. It could then be attacked from all sides and exhausted.

Could Canada have been saved by France? We have mentioned that King Louis XV kept many tens of thousands of excellent troops in Europe to fight his other enemy, Frederick the Great of Prussia. Do you think that these men under Montcalm's leadership could have saved the day for the French in Canada? If you look carefully through the chapter on New France, you will notice that Canadian farming could only just support the 50,000 settlers. Imagine what would happen to the food situation if 50,000 troops suddenly arrived!

So Montcalm and Vaudreuil faced a crushing superiority in numbers. Montcalm saw that a defensive struggle was the best one. This meant that he set himself the task of avoiding open battles where the British could use their large numbers to great effect. His victory at Ticonderoga and his three month tussle with Wolfe before the fatal 13th show how right Montcalm's strategy was. But in the end three things gave Britain victory: Pitt's decision to carry on the struggle to the bitter end; the work of the navy at Louisbourg and in the Quebec channel; and Wolfe's bold and desperate plan on that night of 13 September 1759.

Two names have dominated the last pages of this story. Do you think the British won because Wolfe was a better general than Montcalm? If you want to judge a great military leader then you must see whether he has certain qualities. These are:

1. The ability to face a task honourably and with courage.
2. Good judgment of your enemy's strengths and weaknesses.
3. The ability to produce a plan of campaign which fits the situation.
4. The will-power to put this plan into operation efficiently.

A comparison of the two men will show that there was not much to choose between them.

What about Montcalm? He had to deal with enormous difficulties, and his gallantry has made him a national hero. He did not have the support he should have had from Governor Vaudreuil, or for that matter from the King of France. He certainly comes out very well when measured against the third quality, because at Ticonderoga and at Quebec a defensive campaign was the most intelligent thing to plan. However, Montcalm made two fatal errors. First, he organised and built the defences of Quebec trusting that the British forces would never get up-river above the city. The supplies for Quebec had to come from Montreal and the west by a road which could be cut by an enemy army attacking up-river. Montcalm's second mistake was to attack immediately he found Wolfe's army on the Heights of Abraham. Why he did not wait a few hours for Bougainville's first-class soldiers to arrive is difficult to say. In the chapter which described Montcalm's character I mentioned he was impatient. Perhaps this is the answer; or maybe he dreaded the arrival of more British troops.

What do you think of Wolfe? There have been many books written about him which give him an heroic character. He was a man of great courage and fearlessness, but how about

Brigadier Townshend's caricature of Wolfe. He is comparing Wolfe's domineering personality with the harsh rule of Cromwell a century before

his qualities of leadership as a general? If we test him by our four points, he seems to come out best in the first and fourth. On the Heights of Abraham he played a superb part in leading a big army into action with energy and authority. Like Montcalm, his bravery under heavy enemy fire gave him a high reputation with the men who served under him. But unless you are blinded by hero-worship, you will have to admit that he too had faults. The common soldiers might admire him, but his senior officers and chief advisers at Quebec were very worried about Wolfe's failure to make up his mind and stick to a plan. In July 1759 one officer wrote in his records:

'Within the space of five hours we received three different

orders which were contradicted immediately after their reception, to no small amazement of everyone. I am told he asks no one's opinion.'

Brigadier Townshend was particularly bitter about this last point. Have a look at the *caricature* of Wolfe he drew, on page 99. Brigadier Murray, who stayed on in Canada to become its first Governor-General, had a long-lasting hatred for Wolfe. In 1774, he wrote to a friend:

> 'I am knocking my obstinate Scotch head against the admiration and reverence of the English mob for Mr Wolfe's memory.'

Do you think such views were fair, or were these men just jealous? Shall we be fair, and leave the last word with Wolfe himself? He once wrote in a letter:

> 'Experience shows me that in war something must be allowed to chance and fortune, seeing that it is in its nature hazardous and an option of difficulties; that the greatness of the object should come under consideration; and that the honour of one's country is to have some weight.'

H.M.S. Centurion, *a 60-gun ship-of-the-line*

17 The Deaths of Wolfe and Montcalm: the Painters' View

The photographs on pages 102 and 103 are from two contemporary paintings, and so you might expect them to be accurate in their detail. Look carefully at those present. In Edward Penny's painting there are four main figures; in Benjamin West's painting of Wolfe's death there are thirteen. Who, if either, was right? Here then is a problem for you. If you saw two pictures painted of some great event by two artists living at that time, and you noticed that the two pictures disagreed, how would you try to find out which was correct?

The way to start is to look for written accounts, and obviously the best evidence will be by eye-witnesses. In the case of Wolfe's death the fullest contemporary account was by Captain John Knox. His story has been checked by many people and found to be the most accurate. Knox went to great trouble to collect information about Wolfe's last moments, and what he said proves Penny's picture to be better history. Edward Penny was a professor at the Royal Academy and exhibited his 'Death of Wolfe' in 1764. As you can see, it shows the dying Wolfe lying on the ground, supported by a soldier, Volunteer Henderson, kneeling behind him. On the general's right kneels another person—a 'private man', Knox calls him—who is wiping Wolfe's face'. Lieutenant Browne of the Louisbourg Grenadiers stands pointing towards the field of battle in the distance. A figure on the left waving his hat is running towards the group, probably announcing victory.

Benjamin West was an American artist who settled in London at the end of the war, and in 1771 exhibited his 'Death of Wolfe', one of the most famous of all historical paintings. An engraving from it sold thousands of copies in London, Paris

Benjamin West's 'Death of Wolfe'
Key
1. General Wolfe. 2. Surgeon Adair. 3. Captain Hervey Smith. 4. Lieutenant Henry Browne of Louisbourg Grenadiers. 5. Sir William Howe. 6. Brigadier Robert Monckton. 7. Grenadier Henderson. 8. Lieutenant-Colonel Fraser. Only 4 and 7 are known to have been present.

and Vienna, and prints brought in £15,000 by the end of the century—a great deal of money in those days. The popular imagination had been captured.

Yet West's picture is not true to history. Let us examine it closely. It represents the dying Wolfe surrounded by a group of high-ranking officers, with a kneeling Cherokee Indian gazing at the general. In reality the written records show that most of these officers were engaged on the battlefield: Monckton, another of Wolfe's brigadiers, was lying badly wounded himself elsewhere; the kneeling officer has the face of Robert Adair (you may have heard of the song 'Robin Adair') but army records show he was never at Quebec, nor even in America! West is known to have asked Murray to allow him to include his portrait, but Murray refused. Also another

Edward Penny's 'Death of Wolfe'. Lt. Browne is standing and Grenadier Henderson is behind Wolfe.

senior officer was asked by West to pay him £100 for the privilege of forming one of the group. He refused. Perhaps Murray's absence but the presence of the other officers has something to do with such money matters! To put the Indian in the picture was a great mistake. Not only was it inaccurate, but it shows how little the artist knew about Wolfe, who disliked Indians intensely and certainly never commanded any. It has come to light since that West took the Indian figure from an eighteenth-century painting of Niagara Falls—he copied the exact pose, even to the musket which rests across his thigh.

So two problems remain: why did West paint an inaccurate picture, and why was it so successful? In answer to the first, and also to give West some credit, it was deliberately done to make the picture an impressive memorial of heroic death. Remember the ground was well prepared, for Wolfe was a popular hero. West composed his painting with two things in mind. First, he put in a large number of figures with mixed expressions on their faces with the idea of drawing the person looking at the painting into the circle of mourners; the person would have sympathy with one of them. (Note the impersonal grief of the grenadier standing on the right with clasped hands, the anxious face of the surgeon wiping Wolfe's brow, the unknowing eagerness of the soldier running up with news of victory, the indifference on the face of the Indian.) Secondly, West composed the picture on the traditional lines of the many versions painted through the ages of the *passion* of Christ. In doing this he hoped to link Wolfe in people's imagination with the emotions of awe and grief which the religious paintings have inspired in Christians for centuries. The enormous sale of prints of his picture shows how successful West was.

So a picture which could have become a laughing-stock because of its wild errors became a success. The people at that time did not know the details of the Quebec campaign, and remember that, unlike today, there were few newspapers keen on investigating such matters. Anyway, West was very lucky: the king, George III, liked West's painting; when this became known, you can imagine that 'The Death of Wolfe' had a big sale.

A Frenchman named Vatteau was so impressed by the success of West's picture that he quickly produced one of Montcalm's death. This was even more inaccurate than West's. He made Montcalm die on the battlefield; and, as decoration, around a group of figures he put in some palm trees! There are no palm trees in a climate such as Quebec's, and, as we have seen, Montcalm was only wounded on the field of battle.

HOW DO WE KNOW?

Building up the accurate details of a complicated story can be a difficult but interesting and exciting task. If you want to know what a particular regiment or ship did on a certain day, then you must look for the official records (log books etc.) in the many places where they are kept. In London there is the Public Records Office, in Canada the Public Archives. These will give you only part of the story. What if you want to know why something was done, or what it was like actually to be there at an event? Then you would have to search through the many contemporary accounts that still exist. I have made many references to Captain John Knox in this book. He kept a journal (a sort of long diary) of the 'Campaigns in North America' which was published first in 1769; the present edition is in three huge volumes, and they give a great wealth of information. An American university has the original of Wolfe's Journal.

But you must not be satisfied with just one account. Obviously Knox did not give the French point of view; so you have to look for the letters and diaries of the leading French soldiers. Montcalm kept a journal, and Governor Vaudreuil's letters are in print. These sources put some flesh on the rather dry bones of the official documents; the personal stories and opinions show us what people who were present thought and felt.

Such things are called by historians 'primary sources'—that is, first hand. Other books are called 'secondary sources'; they are descriptions by many different people writing long after the events and using the primary sources. So far this might seem straightforward, but there are still problems to solve. Two of these problems make the true story of the struggle for Canada especially interesting.

The first problem concerns the myths and legends of the Quebec campaign. The story of the victory was full of drama: the towering fortress at Quebec, the dark river, the night climb, the brief encounter on the Heights, the deaths of Wolfe and Montcalm. Is it any wonder that numerous legends have grown up. Legends make good stories, but they are not history. Take, for example, the famous night encounter between the early boats and the French sentries, described on page 88. According to the legend, the French-speaking Highland officer not only said 'La France', but added the words 'de la Reine'—that is, he gave the name of his regiment. In 1959 a Canadian Army historian, Colonel Stacey, thought this worth looking into, and by some careful checking found that the Regiment de la Reine was hundreds of miles away on the shores of Lake Champlain. So much for that two hundred-year-old story!

The second problem is what to make of the violent disagreements about the various people in the stories that have arisen since those days. Ask yourself the question, was Wolfe a hero? If so, was he and is he still a hero to everyone, including the French-Canadians of today? If not, then how do you explain why he is more famous than the other important men like Saunders and Amherst? Some writers are great admirers of Wolfe; others have serious questions to ask about his ability. Re-read the chapter on Quebec and see how much luck Wolfe had. Remember also that for a century or so after 1759, English-speaking Canadians saw that date as the real beginning of Canadian history:

'In days of yore from Britain's shore
Wolfe, the dauntless hero, came,
And planted firm Britannia's flag
On Canada's fair domain.'

Yet French-speaking Canadians still sometimes feel that Canadian history came to an abrupt halt in 1759.

One man, an American named Francis Parkman, decided to tell the full story, and in 1884 he published a huge book called 'Montcalm and Wolfe'. It had over 700 pages, and Parkman had taken about forty years to collect the facts. It is perhaps the best of what I called the secondary sources, but even a good account like this has its drawbacks. In finding out the true story you must remember that some writers are biased. The word *bias* is a difficult one, but nonetheless a very important one for historians: if you are biased you are prejudiced or influenced by a particular point of view. Parkman told a wonderfully exciting story, but he was an American and a Protestant. He disliked the French-Canadian way of life, because it was Catholic and feudal. I hope I have shown you in the chapter on New France that things were different there, but that does not mean that the English colonies were better than New France.

Some details of the past cannot be discovered by looking for written sources. So archaeology comes to the aid of history. For instance, Fort Ticonderoga played an important part in the story. Montcalm won his finest victory there over the blundering Abercrombie; a year later Amherst captured a blazing fort. After the American Revolution (1775–83) the fort lost its military value, and was soon abandoned. It became a stone quarry for the new settlers moving into the region. Within a hundred years only grass-covered earth was to be seen. In 1908 a local landowner, Stephen Pell, thought he would try to restore the fort. It is today completely reconstructed, and in it there is a vast military museum of cannons, flintlocks and other equipment found in the excavations, birch-bark canoes, old maps and American Indian equipment.

THINGS TO DO AND WRITE ABOUT

1. Write a conversation between a Virginian planter and a *seigneur* of New France, in which the Virginian explains how he would go about making New France more prosperous and the seigneur defends his quiet rural way of life.
2. Plan and construct a model of an Iroquois long-house.
3. Construct a model of Fort Ticonderoga, using the photograph, diagram and description in the book.
4. Work out the arguments FOR his way of life as a *coureur de bois* saw it and AGAINST as the Intendant of New France might see it.
5. The story of Wolfe's siege of Quebec and the final battle has been written mainly from the British point of view. Imagine you are a French officer, and using only the facts given in the book, tell the events from his point of view.
6. Washington at Great Meadows, Braddock at Duquesne, Abercrombie at Ticonderoga all failed against the French; Dieskau at Lake George, Drucour at Louisbourg, Montcalm at Quebec all failed against the British. Work out why each failed to win, using the following headings: Size of army, Equipment and arms, Qualities of soldiers and senior officers, Strategy before battle, Tactics on battlefield.
7. If you were a war reporter which of the eight battles in this book would you most liked to have covered? Write your choice up as a modern newspaper would require: work out headlines, subheading, introductory paragraph in large print, detailed account of events. Consider carefully the excitement, the danger, the human interest, the importance of the victory.
8. As an interviewer you were allowed to ask the following three questions of Montcalm just before he died:
   (*a*) Why did you not provide a better guard at the Anse au Foulon?
   (*b*) Why did you attack Wolfe before Bougainville arrived?
   (*c*) Why did you not train your men better?
   What answers do you think he would have given?
9. Construct a chart showing the different ways of life of the English settlers, the French settlers and the American Indians. Use columns like: how governed, how living earned, social life, dress, marriage, housing etc.
10. Describe a typical day in the life of a habitant.
11. Draw or paint (*a*) one of the battle scenes which appeals to you most; (*b*) a scene either out-of-doors or inside the seigniory during the Mai Day' celebrations (see page 15).

GLOSSARY

abatis, defence made of tree-tops and branches
aigrette, jewelled ornament or plume
baronial seat, country mansion and estate
bastion, tower at the corner of a fort
bias, prejudice or one-sided viewpoint
bodkin, comb for dressing the hair
Brown Bess, nickname given to musket—origin uncertain
to capitulate, to surrender
caricature, drawing exaggerated to make a person look ridiculous
carnage, slaughter of a large number of people
coureur de bois, bush trapper
debauched, spoilt by too much eating and drinking
debouched, rushed out from a small space
demi-lunes, outworks of a fort
frigate, swift ship with about thirty-five guns on one gun-deck only
galley, low-built ship using oars; forced labour in one was common as a punishment
habitant, Canadian peasant and tenant
indigo, violet dye from the leaves of the indigo plant
indocile, not easy to manage
infatuated, acting without thinking as though hypnotised
irregular, soldier not trained by a government
militia, men drilled as soldiers, but usually for local service only
morale, pride and enthusiasm in an army
notorious, widely-known to everybody
party-coloured, patches of different colour
Passion, the suffering of Christ at the Crucifixion
plausible pretext, reasonable excuse
primæval, very ancient; the ages before man on earth
redoubt, small military defence, a field-work
regular, permanent, professional soldier—i.e. not the militia
rout, fuss and bother
sachems, important Iroquois chiefs
scapegoat, someone made to take the blame for another's mistakes
seigneur, Canadian landlords, the gentry; *seigniory*, his house
ships-of-the-line, normally big ships with fifty to hundred guns
speculator, man who buys and sells at a big risk
strategy, grand plan of attack
Traverse, narrow river passage of the St Lawrence between dangerous sandbanks
unbridled, savage and unrestrained

British Colonies and New France

circa 1750

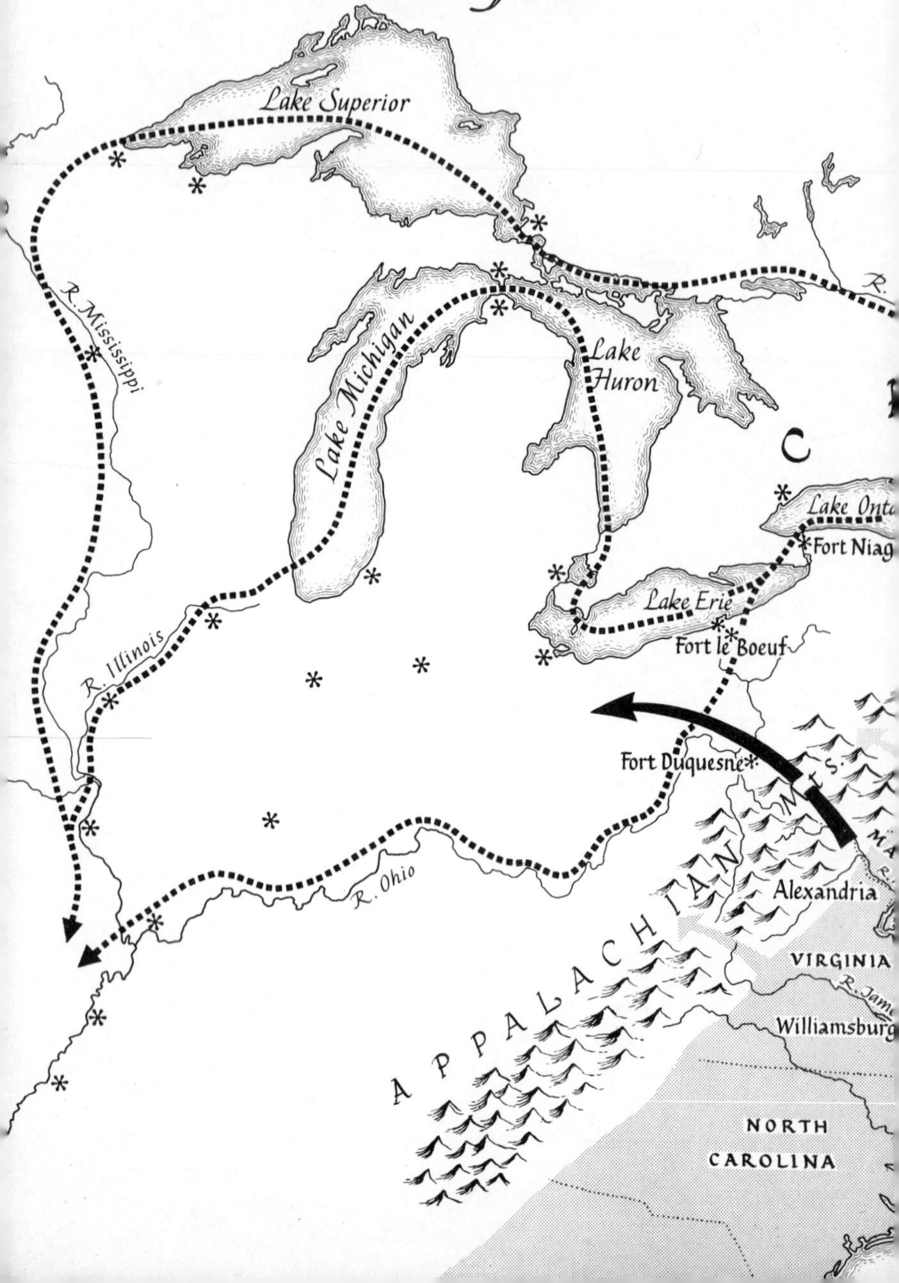

Lake Superior
R. Mississippi
Lake Michigan
Lake Huron
C
Lake Onta
Fort Niag
Lake Erie
Fort le Boeuf
R. Illinois
Fort Duquesne
MTS.
R. Ohio
APPALACHIAN
Alexandria
VIRGINIA
R. Jame
Williamsburg
NORTH
CAROLINA
R.
MA